HOMETOWN

Frc

BURNET, TX

1929-1939

The 1874 courthouse, pictured around 1900

By John Hallowell

Editor: Lindsay Inscore Hallowell

ACKNOWLEDGMENTS

This book is just the second that I have written, and it is a memorable project for many reasons. For one, I have often told people that "I discovered my hometown when I moved to Burnet." My family and I received a very warm welcome when we arrived in 1996, and my experiences there formed the foundation for my excellent 20-years-plus adventure in the publishing business.

During my time in Burnet, I was privileged to serve on historical commissions for the city and county of Burnet with two inspirational historians (and personal friends). We lost Carole Goble and Darrell Debo in 2019, but I am deeply indebted to them, and I dedicate this book to their memory. Knowing them and reading their writings has provided rich material and personal motivation for my own writing. This book is partly theirs.

I thank Karl Piehl, Texas Parks and Wildlife, and others who have helped me find historical photos to illustrate this book.

I also have to thank the readers and advertisers of the *Highland Lakes Weekly* (who supported me as I wrote the book, one chapter at a time, as articles for the paper); also the friendly and helpful staff at the Herman Brown Free Library (where nearly all my research was done).

And I want to thank all those who purchased (and complimented) my first book: *Lake LBJ and the Re-Birth of Kingsland*. Their positive response gave me the confidence to proceed with this second huge project. I expect that my books will have a much longer shelf-life than my newspapers and magazines, and that they will be more valuable in the long term to the communities I write about.

John Hallowell

TABLE OF CONTENTS

PREFACE

The *Burnet Bulletin* (published continuously since 1873) provided world news along with local events (including items about illnesses, travels and weather) during the decade between 1929 and 1939; microfilm archives available at the Herman Brown Free Library provided a fascinating on-the-spot look at times past in Burnet, and were the source for almost everything in this book.

While I never had the opportunity to MEET Publisher L.C. Chamberlain, I feel like I became quite well acquainted with him while reading eleven years of his writings. His optimistic outlook and his conversational style endeared him to me and made my research much more enjoyable than it otherwise might have been. He is officially now one of my literary heroes.

Even with such a good source, there were problems in turning "current events" into "history." Many of the streets were still not named in 1939; street numbers were apparently not even thought of. This makes it difficult to give a definite location of many business buildings, but there was an abundance of clues in the newspaper articles I referenced that would help a serious researcher decide where many of the businesses were located. Many of the buildings are still standing, and a glimpse of their history makes a tour of downtown Burnet much more interesting. I have tried not to make any guesses, but to just present the clues as I found them in the stories of the time.

Several names (of people, places and businesses) appeared in different forms in different news items; I tried to copy each story as it appeared, except for obvious typographical errors.

All in all, I think that what I have been able to put together in this book is interesting and educational (it certainly has been for me!). It is NOT the be-all and end-all of Burnet history, even for the eleven years I studied; a serious historian would want to have more precise sources and more complete details. But I hope you'll enjoy my book (and learn a little about this wonderful town) in spite of all its shortcomings.

John Hallowell

CHAPTER ONE

BURNET BEFORE

Samuel Holland was the first permanent "settler" in Burnet. The former Texas Ranger came to visit his brother-in-law, William B. Covington, at a Ranger encampment a few miles south of present-day Burnet. He liked the surroundings so much that he bought 1,280 acres on Hamilton Creek in 1848 and built a home there.

At the time, most of the Texas Hill Country was uncontested Comanche territory, but in 1849, Army dragoons built Fort Croghan (named in honor of Colonel George Croghan, a hero in the War of 1812) to protect settlers at the edge of the wild frontier. A village called Hamilton was established in the shadow of the fort. Although Fort Croghan was abandoned in 1853, as the frontier continued to move westward, the little village survived and grew into a small town.

Two veterans of the Texas Revolution played major roles in the growth of the new town. Logan Vandeveer was a large and powerful man, known for his courage and daring; Peter Kerr was better known for his business acumen. Vandeveer fought the Indians and supplied the fort with beef and other supplies; Kerr bought the land which eventually became Burnet and donated 100 acres to the county (formed in 1852) to make Hamilton the county seat. Vandeveer was the town's first postmaster and built the first rock building in 1854; Kerr won fame as a benefactor to the poor and a promoter of education in his little town. The name of the town was changed to Burnet in 1858 to avoid confusion with another Texas town already named Hamilton.

1

In the meantime, a young Kentucky native named Adam Rankin Johnson had arrived in 1854, seeking to make his fortune as a surveyor. He married a girl from Austin and built a large rock house by Hamilton Creek in 1860. Although he left the following year for a legendary career in the Confederate Army, he returned and worked for most of the next six decades (even though he had been blinded by a musket ball during the war) to promote the town.

It was the arrival of the railroad in 1882 that turned the small frontier outpost into a boomtown, and many of the buildings around Burnet's square were built during the 1880s. Oxcarts hauled goods from the Burnet railroad depot to towns around the Hill Country, and all kinds of businesses were built along Burnet's busy streets. The town was incorporated as a city in 1883, but the boom died down when the railroad was extended to Marble Falls, Llano and Lampasas; Burnet remained an established little city, but there wasn't much change between 1890 and 1930.

One notable exception was a beautiful new school, described as "Burnet's Pride," completed in 1898. It was a three-story building of white limestone, with blue granite steps; all the materials had been quarried within a mile of town. It had seven large classrooms for its 300 students, plus a third-floor auditorium capable of seating "700 or 800 persons." The top of the bell tower was 75 feet above the ground, making it the tallest building in Burnet's history.

The school superintendent was Professor R.J. Richey, who had graduated from Washington & Lee University in Virginia, and who had served as a pallbearer at the funeral of General Robert E. Lee. Professor Richey did such a good job with the school system in Burnet that wealthy citizens from all over West Texas sent their children to Burnet schools. Another well-known Burnet resident was attorney Dayton Moses, who was famous for his oratory and reportedly was considered at one time as a possible Democratic nominee for president.

Dozens of small farming communities dotted the Burnet County landscape back then, and the more-recently-formed towns of Bertram (1882) and Marble Falls (1887) were growing, but (in addition to being the county seat) Burnet was still the biggest and most influential town in the county. Unfortunately, most of the "modern conveniences" had not arrived in Burnet before 1930, and the little

This limestone schoolhouse was "Burnet's Pride" when it was built in 1898.

city's infrastructure was primitive at best.

A 1928 issue of the *Burnet Bulletin* contained an interview with J.H. Stapp, a long-time resident and well-known merchant in Burnet. Here are some excerpts which give some insight into daily life in Burnet during the 1920s:

"Not many years ago, electric service in Burnet after 11 p.m. meant that someone was sick. For in those days only by special arrangement with the light plant was the service maintained after that hour, and nothing less than sickness was sufficient reason for the extra expense and labor that continuation of lighting caused.

Burnet was a great place in the early days. I well remember when the courthouse was a little wood structure on the far end of the square, and there were but a few other buildings to be found around the town. In those old days, we used tallow candles for our night time activities around the house, and when the oil lamps came in it was a revelation to us. Of course, oil was rather expensive in those times, for it had to be hauled many miles before we could use it, and when we first got it, we were in constant fear that the lamps would explode on us."

This little power plant, built by W.C. Galloway around 1916, provided all the electricity Burnet had in the early 1900s. Mr. Galloway was the mayor of Burnet through most of the 1930s.

"We got along just fine for years with this arrangement, and read as best we could with the yellow rays of the lamps shining in the room. And then there came another revelation to us. About ten years ago, this was. W.C. Galloway put up his electric light plant and ran wires around the square to serve the business houses and a few residences. He figured that we should all be in bed by 11 o'clock at night, so at that hour, the lights blinked a few times and then went out until the next evening at dark. I know as an undertaker that I had to work many times at night, and whenever I knew that I would be up on the job late I had to notify the plant for an extension of service. At times, when something would happen down at the plant, we didn't have service for three or four days at a time. But we were mighty glad to get electricity, and Mr. Galloway did a mighty fine job in serving us.

Then Burnet, as most progressive towns, progressed to the point where it felt expansion of its industries and the need of greater electric power, so the plant was sold to the Texas Power & Light company. Now we are in a position to operate the biggest motors that we want to. In our homes, we can have electric ranges and electric refrigerators, and use all the electric irons and electric heating fans without fear of blowing out the lines in our homes."

That was the situation in Burnet at the beginning of 1929, when this book takes up the tale of an unsuspecting Texas town about to enter America's "Great Depression" (and the roller-coaster ride of those tempestuous years).

CHAPTER TWO

Burnet in 1929

As the Roaring Twenties came to an end, businesses in Burnet issued messages of optimism for 1929 by way of ads in the January issues of the *Burnet Bulletin*. The ad from LaForge Hardware said "Before us lies a new year of opportunities. Let us all make the most of this bright business outlook." Similar ads came from Burnet Cream & Produce Co., Churchill Hardware Store, Guthrie-Howell Co. ("the store that supplies the home," advertising "Hawk" brand work clothes), Roy Fry's Drug Store, Burnet National Bank, Charles G. Fisher's Magnolia Filling Station (with "anti-knock" gasoline), the Green Parrot Coffee Shoppe, the Burnet Filling Station (with "the new TEXACO motor fuel"), Yarborough's Variety Store, J.H. Stapp and the G-H Cash Grocery. Schnabel's Bakery bragged that new equipment had made "a wonderful improvement" in "the quality of our two popular loaves," and Texas Power & Light urged customers to "make 1929 the most active year that Texas has ever experienced."

Guthrie-Howell offered specials at the next "Trade Days" event, scheduled for January 25 & 26.

But all was not well, and pages were filled with announcements of Sheriff Sales as people apparently were not able to make payments on property and/or taxes.

In February, W. Northington announced that he and Roy L. Walker, who owned several theatres in other towns, would lease the old Lone Star Opera House from owner J.O. Cole "until a desirable theatre building can be secured." He promised that they would refurbish the aging building to "make it comfortable and pleasant during all kinds of weather" and would "present the latest in motion pictures."

Later that month, the *Bulletin* reprinted excerpts from a *Dallas News* article, describing Frank Pavitte's lead mine, "about eighteen miles northwest of Burnet, near the Colorado River and by the side of a mountain near Beaver Creek." The article opined that "the citizens here have good reason to believe that this line of mining will develop to such a degree that the prosperity and population of the town will be greatly increased." The first carload of "lead concentrates" had recently been shipped to the smelter for refining.

An older hotel at the southeast corner of the square was torn down in 1929, and this David G. Burnet Hotel was built to replace it that same year.

A front-page article coyly reported that "Last Thursday, M.W. Nolen of this place was awarded the contract to erect the new modern hotel for Burnet, and started tearing down the old building that afternoon, which work is nearing completion." The writer was probably the owner of the new hotel, *Burnet Bulletin* owner, publisher and editor, L.C. Chamberlain, but that fact was not mentioned in the article. It continued by saying, "The new building will be on the property, across the street southeast from the public square. It will be of stucco and will contain 26 rooms with three additional rooms to the rear of the main building, which will also be of the same material as the hotel proper. It will contain nine bath rooms, one shower, a sewer system, electric lights, a massive front porch, etc. There will be nothing elaborate and unnecessarily expensive in the building, but every thing will be modern, attractive and comfortable. The building will be finished not later than June 1."

The Burnet Furniture Company offered a couple of intriguing items for sale. One was "the greatest oil stove ever built," with prices ranging from $15 to $100. The other was a Crosley All-Electric Radio, fully installed for just $129.50.

A letter to the editor on March 7 (from an 82-year-old Confederate veteran named P.C. Jackson, who had once been a resident of Burnet) contained some very interesting assertions. It started out by saying, "Kerr County is one of the poorest counties in Texas, but Kerrville is a city of 10,000. Burnet County is one of the biggest and best." Mr. Jackson mentioned minerals, railroads, water power and rumors of a dam, which would be "so high that boats will run up to the mouth of the San Saba River." He said that Burnet's courthouse looked like it soon might fall down, and urged residents to prepare for their bright future by building "a fine courthouse." His prediction was that (if the new courthouse was built) Burnet would soon become a major industrial city.

Dickens & Elliott advertised the new 6-cylinder Chevrolet trucks ("with the economy of the four"). The "Dodge Brothers" advertised a new "six" in their cars. Michel & Mezger Ford's ad said, "Simplicity of cooling system is a feature of the new Fords."

A unique ad announced that "Honest Bill and Moon Bros. Combined Shows," with the "most interesting collection of wild animals in the entire world" would be in Burnet on March 12, with a "Big Free Street Parade" at noon. Burnet's event would follow appearances in Bertram on March 9 and in Marble Falls on March 11.

The management of the Lone Star Theatre promised "the very best in motion pictures" six nights a week, and assured their customers that "the house will be made comfortable regardless of weather conditions."

Three business announcements made the front page on March 27.

Clen Shilling had made "some exceedingly attractive and nifty improvements upon his café." George Shaw, of Llano, had contracted to have a new theatre built, which would be "modern, fireproof and up-to-date in every particular." And Robert Wagner, of the Burnet Cream & Produce Company, had "made arrangements to greatly increase the capacity of his cold storage plant."

The rapidly-growing Hokus Pokus grocery chain announced in an ad that week that it would open a new store in Burnet "in the near future." The chain hoped to double the number of stores (100-plus already) and the company's total sales ($80,000,000) in 1929, and Burnet was part of its plan. It offered "chain-store prices," quick and easy check-out and optional free delivery as keys to its success.

The Green Parrot Coffee Shoppe served a banquet on March 26 for veterans of the Spanish-American War.

On April 11, the *Bulletin* announced that E.E. Greathouse (from Goldthwaite, where he had worked at his father's "two modern gins") had purchased the old Brooks gin and was in the process of tearing it down to build a new gin ("modern in every respect") in Burnet. The article ended by saying, "A modern gin, a modern hotel and a modern picture show" were "all going up at the same time in Burnet."

LaForge Hardware placed an ad for Nesco kerosene cook stoves with the headline, "Throw Your Axe Away!" It claimed many advantages over the wood stoves commonly in use at the time.

The April 18 paper reported that a new law would go into effect on June 14, requiring couples wishing to get married to apply three days in advance to get a marriage license from the county clerk. The headline said, "Not so easy to marry after June 14."

The ad for Hokus Pokus announced that it would open its new grocery store "next door to the post office" on Saturday, April 27. The ad also said "SUGAR FREE!" in large letters, but the words had a different meaning in 1929; the store was offering a free pound of sugar with each pound of coffee purchased (limit 3 pounds).

The Burnet County Wolf Club announced that, since its formation in 1925, it had killed not only 52 wolves and 22 wolf pups, but 343 "wild cats," all of which would otherwise be killing sheep and goats in Burnet County. J.C. Morrow and W.J. Daugherty earned $207 for bringing in a whole family of wolves (two adults and five pups) from a ranch ten miles west of Burnet.

Wimpy's Grocery advertised "Specials for Saturday," including "fresh berries on ice." Ernest Craddock's Burnet Filling Station advertised Goodyear Double-Eagle Tires, and Burnet Cream & Produce announced that its "Ice Wagon goes out every morning. Get your cards out early!" Simpson & Bowmer's City Meat Market advertised "All Kinds of Fresh and Cured Meats."

At the end of May, L.C. Chamberlain advertised "a large amount of second-hand lumber" for sale at very reasonable prices at the Burnet Hotel building site. The *Bulletin* commended Robert Wagner for the improvements at his cold storage plant; the ice house could now hold "more than 100,000 pounds of ice." On the north side of the building was "a room for storing and candelling eggs, and for the storage of sour cream." There was also a "machinery room, where he will make and harden cream, and which has sufficient space to hold 150 gallons."

High school students organized a Saturday "Carnodeo," which consisted of a parade (featuring an "old-time schooner wagon pulled by a team of mules"), a mini-rodeo, a carnival and a baseball game. Nila Hallmark was crowned "Queen," and Wilbern Garrett was King. The event was considered a huge success.

A contest was being held to name the new theater in Burnet, and the June 13 *Bulletin* reported that more than 100 suggestions had been turned in. The prize was $5 in gold.

A June 20 article reported that the Syndicate Power Company expected to soon reach an agreement to build dams (plural) on the Colorado River above Austin and continued, "Among the earliest results of Syndicate Power activities will be the completion of the Marble Falls cotton mill, which is being delayed because of the river water controversy."

The new Hokus Pokus store reported (in an ad) that it had purchased "a perfectly good Ford and a telephone" to follow through with their promise of free delivery. To reassure hesitant customers, Hokus Pokus offered a money-back guarantee on every item in the store. The ad listed E.D. Maxwell as the store manager.

A "Grand Celebration" was announced at Enchanted Rock, in southern Llano County, for Saturday, June 22. Governor Dan Moody was to be the keynote speaker, and an automobile was expected to climb the rock; a "glorious dance" was planned for that night, and 5,000 people were expected to attend.

The June 27 paper noted that Bunk Gibbs was "engaged in making valuable and attractive improvements in his store building." Among them was the installation of a metal ceiling and walls of sheetrock, which would "make the inside of the building practically fire-proof."

On June 28, the new "Burn-Tex" theater was opened to the public, and a large crowd was on hand for the occasion. Mrs. Debo was the first of several to suggest the chosen name, and she received a $5 gold piece for her winning suggestion. The theater's short-term plans were to show movies on Monday, Tuesday, Friday and Saturday evenings, with a "comedy and a news-reel" to open each show.

The July meeting of the Burnet Chamber of Commerce was mainly devoted to planning the annual Chamber Banquet, which was to be held on the lawn of the new Burnet Hotel (weather permitting). Adam R. Johnson Jr. would be the toastmaster, and Governor Dan Moody would be the keynote speaker; live music would be provided by the Llano Municipal Band.

An "important meeting" was to be held in Burnet on July 23, with interested citizens "from Austin to Mason" invited to provide input in the planning of the new Highway 29.

Two building projects made the front page of the *Burnet Bulletin* on the first week of August, 1929. Mr. H.B. Duncan had hired contractor M.W. Nolen to tear down the old Tarver Brothers Garage on the west side of the square and build "an up-to-date garage building" in its place. The structure would be 45' x 70' with plate glass windows in a stuccoed front. It would be in between Shilling Confectionery (on the south side) and John H. Olney (on the north). The building would feature "a ladies rest room and other conveniences."

The other story was Burnet's new cotton gin, which was "modern in every respect," and had cost "thousands of dollars" to equip with the latest machinery.

In a very personal front-page column in September, publisher L.C. Chamberlain told how he had come to Burnet in 1901. "We could rent the best residence in town for $5 per month, and our advertising patronage was less than one tenth what it is today."

"The people have been good to me," he continued. "I like all of them, and I believe most of them like me." "All of my children were born here in Burnet, and I like the place better than any spot on earth." "I hope to be with the people of Burnet County many more years, doing my mite as the editor of the *Bulletin*, and when the time comes for me to pass on, I trust that my posterity will continue the publication of the paper with the same pleasure that such has been to me for the past 28 years."

State Highway engineer Bouldin Crofton came to Burnet in September to visit with Mayor Willis Smith and members of the Chamber's road committee about the proposed south-to-north "Air Line Highway." Two possible routes through Burnet were discussed: one between the square and the depot and one between the square and Hamilton Creek (since Main Street was too narrow to meet the highway department's 100-foot requirement). The city of Burnet would have to "furnish the right-of-way through the corporation" if it wanted the highway to pass through the town. The *Bulletin* was very much in favor of having the highway come through town "if the expense does not appear prohibitive."

On October 3, a small front-page item reported that approximately $80,000 had been invested in buildings and improvements in Burnet since the beginning of the year. The *Bulletin* opined that "Burnet is rapidly coming into its own, and shows a very beautiful financial condition. Next year, if conditions are as the *Bulletin* is led to anticipate, improvements and building will surpass even this year."

A Saturday "Trade Day" event drew "immense crowds to Burnet from every section of the county, and from adjoining counties." The *Bulletin* credited ads in its pages, and noted that "such bargains were offered that the people could not let the opportunity pass of purchasing a goodly portion of their fall and winter supplies." Merchants reported strong sales, and Guthrie-Howell (the leading department store in Burnet, located at the southwest corner of the square) had "the third-greatest day in its history."

Not all the news was good; a midnight fire in early October destroyed "the large stone building across the street north of the Burnet Lumber Company" with all its contents. The lumberyard was saved by the fact that manager T.O. Whitaker had "several barrels of water handy and a bucket brigade was formed and kept things wet until the danger was over." The building contained goods and wares of different kinds. The Burnet Furniture Company's old hearse was burned, and Mary Ann Pangle lost 11 bales of uninsured cotton. The *Bulletin* noted that the building was "an old Burnet landmark," built around 1885 by "Holloway and Wood."

The Burnet Motor Company, a Ford dealership owned by Pete Elliott and E.J. Kuykendall, opened in the new building on the west side of the square that October.

On October 14, the Chamber of Commerce met to endorse a plan, already under discussion for two years, to build dams along the Colorado River west of Burnet. The article noted that the issue was very controversial, and that the Burnet Chamber had withdrawn from the West Texas Chamber of Commerce because of that entity's bitter opposition to the dams.

The next week's *Bulletin* contained an article reprinted from the *Austin American*, which reported that permits for "five major hydroelectric dams" along the Colorado River in Travis, Burnet and Llano Counties had been sold by Power Syndicate Co. to Chicago financiers Emery, Peck and Rockwood. The new permit owners were "engaged in securing options on overflow rights for the uppermost dam near Kingsland."

The article went on to say that Samuel Insull, of "the Insull power interests," had withdrawn from the project due to protests by the Brownwood Irrigation District and West Texan interests.

The stock market crash of October 29, 1929, went unreported in Burnet, and the largely agriculture-based economy of central Texas did not immediately feel the ripple effects of the growing depression. The biggest issue facing Burnet at the end of 1929 was the planned location of two new highways through the town. In an article titled "Problems to Face," the *Bulletin* noted that "the Airline Highway will pass through the county and town, and whatever route it may take, it will require a right-of-way through the property of a number of people." "The same condition exists among property owners on the Colorado who own land that will be covered by water." The article concluded by noting that most locals favored both projects and that "we may rest assured, whether that is any comfort or not, that we will be paid what the property is worth, and when the route is decided upon, it will go that way whether we are pleased or not."

Louis Wagner placed an ad in November, announcing that he

had opened "The Cash Grocery" in the old Burnet Cream & Produce building. He said, "I will assure you a square deal, quality merchandise and prompt service. I will buy your eggs, butter, or anything you have in that line. Will pay cash and sell for cash."

Also in November, a small article appeared under the headline "Burnet will go into the New Year with bright prospects." It cited the planned dam and Air Line highway, two lead mines, and a quantity of "ichthyol" deposits north of city limits as positive factors.

On December 5, the *Bulletin* reported that "Mr. Shaw" had made arrangements to install a "non-synchronous" sound machine at the Burn-Tex Theatre so patrons would "hear all of the latest theme songs in connection with a perfect cue to all the latest photoplays." It would be ready for the December 12 presentation of "Broadway Babies," an "all talking, singing and dancing picture."

The headline on December 12 said, "Permit for dam below Marble Falls transferred; new holders expected to develop big project at once." The story reported that Emery, Peck and Rockwood had applied for an extension of the permit to build a dam just one mile "below Marble Falls," which would submerge the existing dam and the power plant at Marble Falls Textile Mills (General Johnson's "factory"), which would be compensated for its loss, and which agreed to purchase power for their looms from the operators of the lower dam).

There seemed to be many reasons for optimism at the end of 1929, but the depression would soon be felt in Burnet County.

CHAPTER THREE

Burnet in 1930

A front-page story on January 9, 1930, reported that "preliminary work for the erection of a huge dam across the Colorado River, a few miles west of Burnet, seems to be progressing in a satisfactory manner."

Many landowners in the projected lake basin had already been paid for their land, engineers were "making necessary surveys," bunkhouses were being built for future employees, and "men with diamond drills from Del Rio" had begun test drills at the future dam site. The *Bulletin* called the project "one of the greatest undertakings of its kind ever started in the United States."

Another article in that week's paper reported that J.E. Landon had been elected president of the Burnet County Fair in Bertram. And another announced the opening of a new chick hatchery in Burnet, located "in the old ice house building at the rear of the *Bulletin* office." It had a capacity of 16,000 eggs.

A "Mr. Johnnie Barnes," from Waco, crashed his airplane at Fall Creek; he and a passenger miraculously escaped severe injury.

At the end of January, the *Bulletin* reported that many old-timers felt that the winter of 1929-1930 had been "the coldest winter within their recollection," with "one of the heaviest snowstorms ever known in this section" in December, and January temperatures as low as four degrees below zero.

The Burnet County Wolf Club announced that payment of bounties would be suspended until more funds were collected.

A news item reported that famous country music singer Jimmie Rodgers would be in Burnet for a live performance at the Burn-Tex Theatre on February 3.

At the beginning of February, editor L.C. Chamberlain told of a visit to the site of the planned dam construction. He reported that "comfortable bunkhouses and other necessary buildings" had been built on the Burnet County side of the river, and a foot bridge ("200 yards or longer") had been built "across the stream," but that "the general public should bear in mind that laborers will not be in demand until actual work on the dam is started."

Another article noted that Congressman R.O. Lee, of Frisco, was urging the federal government to use Texas granite (most of which came from Burnet or Llano County) in its "large public building program." It added that Texas granite had been used in "more than 100 of the large buildings in New York."

The Burnet Motor Company reported that Ford's Endurance and Economy Test, which consisted of driving a new Ford for 8,439 miles around central Texas (including several stops in Burnet) had been completed. The average speed had been 42.62 miles per hour, with 70 being the highest speed reached. The average gas mileage had been 19.8 mpg, and "oil for the entire trip amounted to one gallon and two quarts."

There was some bad news on March 13. The "old H.A. Burns residence, facing the public square in Burnet on the Northwest corner, was destroyed by fire Monday afternoon." The original home, which had been renovated and expanded through the years, had been built before 1880. Mr. Burns had purchased it in 1886, and had lived there until his death a few years before the fire.

Thomas C. Ferguson, an ambitious young Burnet native who studied law at night while working as a linotype operator at the *Bulletin*, declared his candidacy to represent Burnet and Williamson Counties in the Texas State Legislature. He had previously served as Deputy District Clerk and as county chairman for the Democratic Party.

A horse buyer named J.J. McCartney came to Burnet seeking horses between 4 and 7 years old and from 14.2 to 15 hands high for the Filipino government. Horse owners were urged to contact him at the Houghton Brownlee Ranch.

The Norwood & Ferguson Real Estate Company had several interesting listings that spring. One was "350 acres of mountain pasture with cedar timber, springs and running water, in the mineral region 7 miles west of Burnet. $15 per acre." Another was "one stone building on public square in Burnet . . . priced to sell with liberal terms." A third listing was "Lone Star Opera House building and extra lot. Priced to sell quick."

An article at the end of March noted that "with the building of the dams across the Colorado River, west of Burnet, it will be necessary to re-locate the road between Burnet and Llano." The story reported a meeting of the Burnet Chamber of Commerce, where members expressed their belief that the road should follow the Hoover Valley Road to the foot of the mountain, then cross the river below the Arnold Dam.

The Robinson Brothers Bus Line offered "New Low Fares" on routes from Burnet to Austin ($2.25, at 9 a.m. and 5 p.m.) and Burnet to Llano ($1.25, 9 a.m. and 6 p.m.) The Roy Fry Drug Store was the "new bus station."

The Economy Store of Lampasas announced plans to open a Burnet store "at the old Hester building on the west side of the public square."

An old-timer lamented the emptying of the Burnet County countryside, pointing out that only two of the seven homes visible from his front porch were still occupied. He recalled that all seven had been occupied by large families just 20 years earlier, when the county had "a large number of flourishing country schools," averaging 40 to 60 students each. He mentioned the lower birth rate as one factor, and opined that "many people have concluded that farm life is too hard for the returns received."

While the countryside's population may have been declining, the towns were growing. The *Bulletin* reported in May that Burnet County's total population had grown to 10,355 in the 1930 census (an increase of 806 since 1920).

The new Economy Store on the west side of the square announced its Opening Sale, offering a "Complete line of Dry Goods," plus clothing and shoes for the whole family, with "Prices Better than Austin's" for Saturday, May 3. The Burnet Furniture Company advertised Leonard refrigerators ("all steel").

Ray E. Summerow, of the Emery, Peck and Rockwood Development Co., invited those whose family members or friends were buried in the Bluffton Cemetery to meet with him at the Bluffton schoolhouse on May 17. The meeting's goal would be to form a committee which would select a site for a new Bluffton Cemetery (since the old one would be "inundated" when the dam was completed). The company would pay for the site and construction of an entrance and wall, but stipulated that no graves be moved until the construction of the dam was "absolutely assured."

Mrs. Ed Sherrard sold her shop (located next door to the Cowboy Café) to Miss Alba Foulds. Mrs. J.H. Guthrie sold her mercantile business to former schoolteacher Jas. A Box.

Luther Baker, who grew up west of Burnet but was living in San Antonio in 1931, had been walking around his father's ranch during a recent visit when he made an amazing discovery. Living peaceably together in a small cave were two king snakes, two bull snakes, a bullfrog and a house cat mothering the kitten of a wildcat! He surmised that the bitter cold of the previous winter had led them to share the shelter.

The Chamber of Commerce held an unusually well-attended meeting on June 9, and Secretary Willis Smith reported that "forty new names had been added to the membership." Park Commissioner W.A. Kroeger reported that he had persuaded all but one of the "permanent campers" to vacate the city park, and was preparing to clean it up for summer use. Other topics of discussion were a possible "water works" for Burnet and plans for Hwys 29 and 108.

Emery, Peck and Rockwood paid out $125,000 dollars as a final payment to landowners whose property would be submerged by the new lake when Hamilton Dam was completed.

On July 4, a huge crowd attended a barbecue in Bertram. The *Bulletin* reported that "5,000 plates of barbecue were handed out to the visitors, and this did not include all of the great crowd." The keynote speaker was Senator Small, who was running for governor. Games and other festivities followed the political speeches.

M.W. Nolen began renovating and expanding the old post office building (next to the Garrett Hotel on the northeast side of the square), which belonged to W.D. Fry. The building had already been rented to the Burnet Furniture Company for use as a funeral parlor.

The *Bulletin* opined that it would be "a handsome and commodious building" when completed, and added that "Mr. Fry is to be congratulated upon the faith he has in our little city."

A crowd of farmers and curious spectators watched as representatives of the International Harvester Company demonstrated their new Farmall tractor at Captain D.G. Sherrard's ranch. According to the front-page story, "the tractor pulled plowing machinery that plowed an acre of land every 36 minutes, and the work was excellent."

Ed McDaniel, who lived seven miles east of Burnet, brought the first 1930 bale of cotton to Burnet in the middle of July. The bale weighed 545 pounds, and sold the next morning for $54.50. That price was considered very low, but the *Bulletin* pointed out that he also received $60.50 value in premiums offered by local merchants.

At the beginning of August, the *Bulletin* reported that a "small cyclone" had hit Marble Falls at 4 p.m. the previous Tuesday, causing "excitement" all around town. Some residents hid in cellars, but many watched through their windows as the storm approached from the southwest and picked up "a swirling sheet of water" from the Colorado River. Signs were blown down at the Blue Bonnet Café and the Everybody's Cash store; part of a shed roof at Barnes Lumber was blown down. One room at the J.J. Seale home had the windows broken and the wallpaper torn from the walls, but Mrs. Seale and her two children were unharmed in another room. The most extensive damage was at the factory by the river, then owned by Certified Laboratories. Most of its roof was blown away, and about $30,000 worth of equipment was damaged or destroyed. Manager Ernest Remley said the damage would be repaired "immediately," and that he hoped to have the plant producing again by August 15.

Anson Hahn was bitten by a snake while fishing at night on the bank of the Colorado River. He didn't see the snake, but believed that it was a "cotton-mouth moccasin." He hurried to town and had snake serum administered; the *Bulletin* story reported that he had "suffered very severely," but had recovered and was now "a strong believer in snake serum."

Michel & Mezger, of Marble Falls, sold two buildings they had owned on the east side of the Burnet square. Bunk Gibbs purchased the "rock building adjoining his feed store on the south," and J.B. Warden, "of the Oak Hill community," purchased the "two-story rock building in the same block of buildings." Mr. Warden planned to move his family into the upper floor of the building and rent out the street-level storefront. Mrs. J.H. Guthrie purchased the R.B. Norwood place, north of the Burnet Filling Station.

The new funeral home on the north side of the square was ready to open by the middle of August. The *Bulletin* described it as "a very attractive building, 20 by 80 feet, and is partitioned into a state room, an embalming room, a waiting room and a display room."

An August 14 article reported that "the drilling of many hundreds of test holes in the foundation for the dam on the Colorado River near here has been successfully completed." Results showed "a solid granite foundation entirely suitable for the huge dam which is to be built." The time had arrived to seek bids for the actual construction, and the development company expected work to begin quite soon.

An architect's drawing of the new Bluffton Cemetery was released, and the *Bulletin* expressed its view that it would be "the most attractive cemetery in this section of the state." A meeting was scheduled to be held at the Bluffton schoolhouse on September 6 in hopes of forming a cemetery association.

At that meeting, the cemetery committee announced the selection of a six-acre site on the north side of Hwy 29 about three miles east of Lone Grove. Reps of Emery, Peck and Rockwood told the crowd that they would purchase the site and deed it to the cemetery association as soon as it was formed.

A fascinating story from the other side of the world was on the front page of the *Burnet Bulletin* on September 11. It told how Chinese Communists had attempted to break through the defense lines of the city of Changaha by attaching torches to the tails of hundreds of water buffalo and stampeding them toward the city. Machine gun fire from the defenders stopped the charge, and the plan failed. The story stated that there were 40,000 Communists surrounding the city; 17,000 were armed with rifles, but the rest had only spears.

Frank Pavitte reported on September 18 that "the richest lead ore yet" had been uncovered "in gratifying quantities" at his mountainside mine near Beaver Creek.

W.P. Fry began construction on "another residence on his property east of the public square." And one of the large post oak trees at the northwest corner of the courthouse grounds "fell without warning" on September 21, "with no wind at all blowing." No one was injured.

Negotiations were underway at the end of September "to lease Leonard Frazier's rock residence building on Main Street (one block north of the square) and turn it into a hospital." The *Bulletin* was hopeful, noting that "a hospital would fill a long-felt want in this section."

On October 14, Frank Hall killed "the largest rattle snake that many of our citizens had ever seen" at the Sherrard ranch, west of Burnet. While "only" six feet long, the snake had 24 rattles and "its hide was 12 inches wide in the largest place after it had been skinned."

The following week's paper reported that Emery, Peck and Rockwood had hosted "delegations of business men from Austin, Burnet and Llano" at a "splendid dinner" in the dining hall at the construction site for the planned dam. Mr. E.P. Smith, ("connected with the financial division of the corporation in Chicago") told the group that markets were "sluggish" at present, but he expected that "six months will see us enjoying our usual prosperity." Maps of the site were distributed and explained; engineers expected the construction to take two and a half years, with 500 to 800 men working.

An article from the *Austin News* was reprinted in the *Bulletin* on October 28. It predicted that the planned dams would create "one of the greatest series of artificial lakes in the entire United States. It will be one of the greatest hunting and fishing resorts and playgrounds in the entire country." The article noted the benefits for irrigation downstream and the "immense supply of cheap power" that would be supplied by the dam. It also stated that a six-mile-long railroad would have to be built to connect the dam site with "the Llano Branch of the Southern Pacific."

The big news in Burnet on November 9 was the upcoming dedication of Llano's "World War Memorial," a "bronze statue of heroic proportions representing the American Doughboy." Governor Dan Moody would be the keynote speaker at the program, which would begin at 11:30 a.m. on Armistice Day, November 11.

A large ad for "the New Nash" appeared in that week's paper, listing Fred Weber as the "local dealer" (no address given). Nash was obviously an upscale vehicle back in 1931; prices ranged from $795 to $2,025, as compared to around $500 for a basic Ford or Chevrolet.

R.A. Simmons announced that he had purchased the still-new Hokus-Pokus store from E.D. Maxwell; the front-page news item noted that Simmons had been a resident of Burnet for only a few months, but had "gained the esteem and confidence of the people of this community."

In the *Bulletin's* occasional "Texas and Texans" section, a brief item stated that construction in Texas for September had totaled $13,000,000. That figure was up $3 million from August, and was split quite evenly between businesses and residences. Another item recalled that radios had been a startling novelty just ten years earlier, but had since become "the country's cheapest, if not the best form of home education and entertainment." It reported that "a $7 million corporation will likely be formed at San Antonio to manufacture radio receivers."

J.P. Moneyhon opened a new grocery store in Bunk Gibbs' recently acquired rock building on the east side of the square. The Economy Store moved from the Hester building to the Stapp building (on the southwest corner of the square). And the Burnet City Commission made a deal with the State Highway Department, whereby the state would maintain all of Hwy 29 inside city limits except the part "that crosses the public square."

The December 4 paper announced that Burnet Cream & Produce had opened a state-of-the-art turkey dressing plant "capable of dressing from 2,500 to 3,500 turkeys per day," and leaving them "much cleaner and more attractive than when prepared the old way."

The Auxiliary of the Presbyterian Church sponsored a free "Radio Carnival" to be held on the evening of Friday, December 12, at the Lone Star Opera House. The newspaper's description said, "there will be a number of stations 'on the air' and each one will broadcast something of interest to you."

A rare hint of troubled times came in the ad for Wimpy Grocery. It said, "Regardless of our finances, all of us must eat." The City Market's ad, below Wimpy's, just said, "Beef, Pork, Hams, Sausage, Bacon, Dressed Chicken; Cooled by Frigidaire. W.A. Bowmer, proprietor – next door to Schnabel's Bakery – Phone 76 – Burnet, Texas."

A big ad for the David G. Burnet Hotel offered Christmas Greetings. In the middle of its message was this sentence:

"Notwithstanding the general and widespread depression of the past several months, this hotel has prospered far beyond the anticipations of its builders." It credited "home people, the traveling men and those connected with the dam work."

At the end of 1930, Guthrie-Howell (and its G-H Cash Grocery) wished its customers and friends "the brightest and most prosperous year of your lives" in 1931. It had been a tough year for many in Burnet, but there were encouraging signs for future prosperity.

CHAPTER FOUR

Burnet in 1931

The year began with "An Interesting Announcement." Emery, Peck and Rockwood Development Co. announced that "work has been started on construction camps and construction railroad. The camps are on the Llano side of the river. The construction railroad, work on which is now underway, will extend from the dam site to the main line of the Southern Pacific Railroad a short distance above Wood Spur" (about five miles). Bids had already been solicited for the construction of the actual dam, and the deadline was set for January 29, 1931. The land had already been purchased, and the preliminary engineering work had been completed. The company estimated that it would take about 800 employees, working for two and a half years to complete the $6 million project. All the electricity that the dam could produce was already "sold under contract" to Central Texas utility companies.

The Burnet Chamber of Commerce held its first meeting of the year on January 4, and the room was packed with enthusiastic business owners. Of course, the dam was discussed, but "the main topic of conversation was roads." Hwy 108, already completed through Marble Falls to the "South Burnet Precinct line," had come to a stop "in Houghton Brownlee's pasture." And Hwy 29, which would have to be totally re-routed when the dam was completed, was a subject of great interest.

A small news item on January 15 told how Wash Clements had

cleared and cleaned up the Odd Fellows Cemetery so that it was "in the best shape it has been within the memory of our oldest citizens." Another item reported that a nearly disastrous fire at Dan Simpson's house had been put out promptly when volunteer firefighters were directed toward it by the fire siren. That article went on to say that the relatively new siren had already saved hundreds of dollars and "a number of houses."

A fur buyer from Belton was stopped and robbed of "seven or eight hundred pelts of different kinds" about four and a half miles north of Burnet by two armed men in a Ford roadster.

The new Goodman Grocery (in the south end of the Economy Store) reported that, despite rainy weather and muddy roads, their Opening Day had been a big success. Among the specials they advertised were two pounds of prunes for 15 cents, five pounds of peanut butter for 75 cents, and a four-pound bucket of coffee for 85 cents. A one-pound can of salmon cost 13 cents!

A "national news" item reported that "travel abroad" and foreign investments were up considerably despite the ongoing depression. The government had issued 209,211 passports in 1930, up more than 15,000 from 1929.

Burnet Furniture advertised its ambulance and funeral director services, saying, "our hope is that you do not need these services, but should you, we are sure you want the best and the most sympathetic." Their ad showed a fancy black "station wagon" which apparently served as both ambulance and hearse.

Sheriff Andy Ray sold several properties at public auction around February 1, including the property of Southwestern Consolidated Graphite Company and the Bertram Waterwork System. Southwestern Graphite had "operated the graphite mines for a number of years (through 1929) and employed many men. The buyer was the Ceylon Company, one of Southwestern's creditors.

Drs. Charley and Nora Craddock, who had recently graduated from the Texas Chiropractic College in San Antonio, opened an office in Austin.

The February meeting of Burnet's Chamber of Commerce broke all previous attendance records, with 78 members present. The most pressing issue was a road to the dam site, and the consensus was that the best route would be "over the Burnet-Hoover Valley Road to the foot of the mountain, then through the Jim Jones pasture, now owned by Mr. Hallmark, up the river through the Friedman pastures to the Hamilton Dam site." That road was expected to cost about $3,000. Fred Craddock reported that a good landing field, with room for two 1,000-foot runways near "the eastern corporation of the town," had "been secured from J.W. Scott."

Work began the very next week on the road through Hoover Valley to the dam site. A subscription was taken up from the businesses which would benefit from the road, both in Burnet and in Hoover Valley.

Guthrie-Howell, Burnet's leading mercantile firm, closed its doors in February. Attorney Roy Walker, from Lampasas, was "appointed assignee." The *Bulletin* expressed the general regret in Burnet, and the hope that it would soon find a way to re-open. It didn't take long at all; the next week's paper announced that, after a meeting of Guthrie-Howell's creditors, the popular store would "re-open its doors for business on Saturday."

A meeting was announced for representatives of all the towns along the proposed route of Hwy 108 ("from San Antonio to Fort Worth"), to be held in Burnet on March 12. Among the many dignitaries who were expected to attend were Governor Sterling and former Governor Dan Moody.

Guthrie-Howell placed an ad explaining that they were open for business on a cash-only basis, but "you can buy quality merchandise cheaper now by paying cash."

The March 19 paper recapped the "Great Highway Meeting" in Burnet on March 12. The crowd was estimated at 1,500 people, with the largest delegation coming from Lampasas County. Governor Ross Sterling, in his first visit to Burnet County, stressed "the deep responsibility he was feeling toward the people of Texas," and made it clear that he believed that the state should pay for the construction of the highway (through bonds and a gasoline tax) so that locals were not unduly burdened.

The walls of the old rock building ("between town and the depot"), which had burned 18 months earlier, were being torn down "in preparations for some extensive improvements" by owner R.B. Norwood. The building had been built "perhaps 50 years" earlier by Col. F.H. Holloway.

The city elections were held, and 179 people voted. W.C. Galloway was elected mayor, and J.W. Scott and Fred Craddock were elected as commissioners.

L.C. Chamberlain took a tour of the construction site at the dam near the end of March. He reported that "the dump for the railroad was about completed, and some cottages are being erected. The high line from Marble Falls to the dam site is also being erected, and it looks like things are going forward nicely."

Herman Schnabel leased the Burn-Tex Theatre and hoped to have a "talking machine" installed in about 30 days. The *Bulletin* reported that "all are glad the picture show is to be re-opened."

Guthrie-Howell placed an ad in the April 16 paper, listing dress shirts for 50 cents, men's summer suits for $5 to $15, ladies' "Shentung and Crepe" dresses for $3.95 and more.

The April 23 paper announced that the Fegles Construction Company, from Minneapolis, had signed a $3.5 million contract to build the new Hamilton Dam, and that the first trainloads of material should be arriving by train by the beginning of May. That would give the company 22 months to complete the job. The article went on to note that Emery, Peck and Rockwood had already spent $1.3 million dollars in preparations, including buying the land to be submerged and building the new cemetery for Bluffton.

A Ford "truck train" came to Burnet that April, displaying fifteen different types of Ford commercial trucks, including delivery trucks, funeral coaches, ice trucks, dump trucks, police patrols and more.

The State Highway Commission agreed to take charge of completing Hwy 108 into Burnet and connecting it with Hwy 29. Acquisition of right-of-way and other preliminaries were already underway as of April 23, and actual construction was expected to start by May 1.

On April 30, the *Bulletin* reported that "a number of men from Fegles Construction Company" had arrived in Burnet from Minneapolis, and "several carloads of equipment" were on the way. On May 7, a headline said, "Hotels filled to overflowing capacity."

Even though the dam was the biggest story, the construction of new highways (especially the still-undecided route from Burnet to Llano after the dam was built) were topics of "considerable interest" in Burnet.

S.W. Ligon was building a new laundry in Burnet, and the *Bulletin* wished him well in its May 7 edition. Also that week, it reported that Clarence Baker would be in charge of extending Hwy 108 from the Brownlee pasture to Hwy 29 in Burnet, and that work should begin "next Monday" (most of the right-of-way had already been cleared).

Hundreds of strangers had been in Burnet since news of the dam contract had been published, most of them looking for work. The *Bulletin* said that most of them were "doomed to disappointment," since quite a few jobs were already being filled by Fegles employees, and preference was given for the remaining jobs to residents of Burnet and Llano Counties.

By mid-May, a headline reported, "Road to Dam Site More than Half-Way completed," and that it should be ready "by the time the construction people get the bridge across the river at the site." The new road would cut 10 miles from the 25-mile trip on existing roads.

Another mid-May article marveled at the strange weather. "The winters of '29-'30 and '30-'31 will go down in history as the most unusual that any one of the present generation has ever witnessed. The winter of 1929-1930 was undoubtedly the coldest in the past 50 years or longer, and up to the 1st of March, the winter of 1930-1931 was the warmest. But beginning in the first days of March, there has scarcely been a day that it has been comfortable in the evenings without a fire, and northers are coming more frequently in May than they usually do in the dead of winter!" The crops had been harmed, and the writer ended by saying, "the greatest need of this section at the present time is a warm rain followed by hot weather."

Robinson Bus Line offered "excursion rates," with a round trip to Austin at $3 and to Georgetown at just $2.20.

A May 21 article reported rapid progress at the dam site, which was "beginning to look like a little city." The road to the dam site and the temporary suspension bridge across the river at the dam were both coming along nicely.

Mrs. Eliza Guthrie purchased all the assets of Guthrie-Howell Co., and hired L.C. Clark to run her new "Burnet Mercantile" corporation. She was quite well off, owning several farm and ranch properties. She also was a director on the board of Burnet National

Bank. With her backing, the future of the store looked much brighter.

A May 28 article reported that "many people from various sections of the country are camped near the dam site . . . with the hope they may be able to secure jobs." The *Bulletin* pointed out that the company had said repeatedly that local men would have preference in hiring, and opined that many of the campers would be "doomed to disappointment."

Another article reported that "Marble Falls has a jail about completed, and will soon be able to take care of those who go contrary to the law in that community. It will be a substantial building, it is said."

The Fegles Construction Company reported that of 223 men already working on the dam site, only 38 were previous company employees; 185 were from the local area.

Rouse Norwood was nearly finished building a "handsome filling station" "on the street from the public square to the depot," while another was underway "on the northwest corner of the public square," and Lewis Wilson was building still another on the Burnet-Austin road on the east side of Burnet. A building to be used as a restaurant was nearly completed north of the Magnolia Filling Station, and "other improvements in town" were promised soon.

Dr. W.H. Buchanan moved his office into the second floor above Wimpy's Grocery.

Progress continued on the county's roads. Clarence Baker had cleared the right-of-way and brought his equipment to Delaware Creek; his first action would be to build the southern section of Hwy 108 to meet the previously finished road at the Brownlee pasture. The road to the dam site was done "with the exception of causeways and cattle guards, and will soon be open to the public."

A post office was being considered for the Hamilton Dam site, since the hundreds of people there were receiving mail in Burnet, Llano, Bluffton and Kingsland, causing confusion for all.

The Burn-Tex Theatre invited the public to a Grand Opening for talking pictures in Burnet. Herman Schnabel had made a considerable investment in the "talking machine," and was promising "only the best and latest talking pictures." The next week's paper reported that "a large crowd was in attendance" at the first show, and all were well pleased with his initial performance."

E.J. Kuykendall sold the Burnet Motor Company to A.L. Carson, who changed the name to Carson Motor Company.

The weather had improved since May; an article at the end of June reported that "It has been many years since crops of every kind were better in Burnet County."

The Economy Store and Goodman Grocery announced a big sale for July 11. They had bought "thousands of dollars worth of merchandise at bankruptcy prices," and were passing the savings along to their customers. Men's work shirts were 34 cents each, while a pair of work shoes was $1.14. Coffee was 14 cents per pound, and a 48-pound sack of "good flour" was just 98 cents.

W.C. Jackson moved to Burnet from Lampasas to join his brother, T. Jackson, at the Ideal Barber Shop. The O.K. Garage opened on the northwest corner of the square. It was owned by "Messrs. Springer and Wofford, who had recently moved to Burnet from Kansas City." And W.F. Pogue was bitten by a rattlesnake while gathering beans on his farm a few miles north of town. He had been treated with snake serum, and (as of press time) was getting well.

Other news items in the July 16 paper reported that the "cotton flea" was doing considerable damage and that "a large quantity of bottled goods" (tentatively identified as beer) had been "captured by Constable Ham Heffington in Marble Falls." The O.K. Garage advertised their "auto repairing, battery and electric work" "In our new building."

Eight bodies were moved from the old Bluffton Cemetery to the new, and thirty more were to be moved in days ahead as Emery, Peck and Rockwood assessed the difficulties of the operation.

Neuman Bros., from Belton and Georgetown, announced that they had purchased the Economy Store in Burnet, and that Goodman Grocery (previously located in the back of the building) would be closed down.

A mass meeting of Burnet citizens was called for Friday, July 24, to discuss the prospects of creating a "Robert E. Lee Park" at Post Mountain. Mr. O.A. Geddes leased the building just west of the Bulletin office, and was installing "a complete cleaning plant."

Hwy 108 suddenly became Hwy 66, and a meeting of communities along the north-south route was called for August 10 at the St. Anthony Hotel in San Antonio. The temporary suspension bridge at the dam site collapsed as it neared completion; the construction company said that it was because of construction stresses (which "in no way reflected on the stability of the structure as it would be when completed.")

The Burnet Mercantile Company advertised Men's Summer Suits for $2.50 apiece in a special sale. Mrs. Ed Sherrard advertised her "Millinery and Gift Goods," the Cow Boy Café ("L. Debo, proprietor") extended congratulations and best wishes to the builders of the dam, and C.A. Shilling's City Café invited visitors to "Eat and Drink with Us" before going to the dam.

On August 27, the *Bulletin* reported that Burnet had "about 50 active business firms, two splendid school buildings, four substantial church buildings, and good hotel accommodations." The article also mentioned the graphite mines west of town and "the Sheridan copper mines" about seven miles west of town, saying that "hundreds of thousands of dollars" had been spent in their development.

Another article listed several new homes and filling stations under construction (plus a few other buildings) as evidence of economic activity in Burnet, and finished up by noting that demand for housing was "so insistent that scores of our people have cut their residences into apartments."

Waddell Northington bought "the lot east of Will LaForge's home" and started building a new home there. John H. Olney added on to the pressing and cleaning plant at the back of his store. Mr. Thurman Carpenter, from Lampasas, opened another dry cleaning and pressing plant, called City Tailor Shop, "in the old ice building west of the *Bulletin* office."

Texas Power & Light and the Burnet Chamber held a meeting at the end of September to present a plan for re-opening the graphite mine in western Burnet County. With a positive response from most Chamber members, the TP&L representatives stated that the mine could be opened within 30 days, and would employ about 30 workers.

On October 8, a news item was headlined, "Highway 66 is getting close to town." The story predicted that the road would enter city limits "in a short time," but noted that there was still a lot of work in different spots along the road, and that it would still be several weeks before it was completed.

That week's paper also announced that the month just past was "the hottest September on record," not only in Texas, but in "every other state in the Union." A related story said that there had been no rain in weeks, and that vegetation was drying up all around the county.

The next week's paper had a headline, saying, "Highway 66 getting into town," and reported that workers were putting up a bridge "across Hamilton Creek this side of the T.A. Chamberlain farm." That would be the last of the necessary bridges, but there was still "considerable culvert work to do."

This photo shows early stages of construction on "Hamilton Dam," probably taken in the summer of 1931.

F.A. Dale, of Emery, Peck and Rockwood, gave an upbeat report on progress at the dam. Concrete was being poured every day, and more than half of the curved buttresses were already in place. A new highway and bridge were in the works, with the state contributing funds to upgrade the highway from the old road that went through Bluffton.

Also, on October 15, the *Bulletin* reprinted an article from the *Liberty Hill Central Texan*, titled "Highway No. 29 to be Topped Soon." That article concluded by saying, "there is now every reason to believe that arrangements will soon be completed" so the highway in Williamson County "will be widened and topped before the year closes."

A *Bulletin* story on October 22 said, "Those wishing to go to Marble Falls and points south may travel Highway No. 66 the entire distance from Burnet." It continued, "While the road is not completed, it is fair traveling with the exception of only a few places. In coming into Burnet, it has been necessary to move a number of fences, a few barns, a house or two, and to tear down the old Joe Wright blacksmith shop. This building had probably been standing for 50 years or longer."

An ad for an interesting new business appeared on October 29. It said, "NOTICE! We have opened a new shop and will handle a complete line of Popular Records, Atwater Kent Radio and Frigidaire. You are cordially invited to visit our shop and let us demonstrate Atwater Kent and Frigidaire. Burnet Music Co., E.J. Deckert, Mgr. (next door to Fry's Drug Store)."

That week's paper also told of a long-awaited rain in Burnet. An article said, "Breaking a drought of about three months duration, a heavy rain amounting to almost two inches fell at this place last Thursday night. So far as we have been able to learn, it extended throughout the county."

And another article announced that "two new store buildings will be erected in Burnet, on the Walter Wallace property on the east side of the public square." The article concluded by saying, "There is more general improvement going on in Burnet at the present time than in any period during the past 40 years, and such is attracting wide attention to our little city."

A new rental home, under construction by A.F. Shilling, made the news on November 5, as did other homes (under construction or recently completed) by Vernon Greer, Wash Clements, Louis Wilson, Waddell Northington and "a number of other residences in various parts of town." The article ended with the statement that "The town is not on a boom at all, but it is enjoying a very substantial growth."

Another article that week detailed the finishing touches on Hwy 66, and added, "Owing to the very rocky nature of the right-of-way, there was a great deal of difficult work encountered in the building of this road," "This will be by far the best road in Burnet County, and the distance from Burnet to Marble Falls can be traveled in a very few minutes," and "There is talk that the road will be built on through

Burnet and Burnet County soon, but we are unable to state this as a fact."

The *Bulletin* announced on November 12 that Mr. A.L Carson had sold his Carson Motor Company to two men from Taylor, and in an ad the following week, the Smith-Lloyd Motor Company announced "with a great deal of satisfaction" their appointment as the Ford dealer for Burnet. Clarence Hullum was hired to manage the service department, and the new owners invited the public to visit their showroom. They added: "We are prepared to grease your car or truck with the proper oils and grease as recommended by the Ford Motor Co. and at prices surprisingly low."

On November 26, a news item announced, "Hamilton Dam has Post Office." A name for the post office had not been determined, but E.A. Croft had been named postmaster.

On December 3, a fire at the Sinclair Warehouse dominated the news in Burnet. While none of the four large tanks next to the building exploded, the oil and gas inside was consumed by the flames, and black smoke could be seen for miles. Driver Elbert Tippe was filling his truck when the fire broke out, and the truck and his clothing both caught fire. He drove the truck "to a place of safety" before taking the time to extinguish the flames, so the truck was barely damaged.

On December 10, the *Bulletin* encouraged citizens to "Dress up the town for Christmas," and mentioned the large number of visitors the decorations had attracted the previous year.

Burnet's annual Poultry Show was held despite "disagreeable weather" on December 15 and 16, and Walter E. Davis, of Austin, gave tips on raising poultry to the crowd in attendance. M.Z. Glimp and George Hodge also showed colts, and the article ended with the wish that "more colt raising should be done in Burnet County and less automobiles."

"One of the largest crowds ever seen in Burnet" filled "the public square and nearby streets in every direction" on Christmas Eve in 1931. Burnet merchants, who together had offered a new car for raffle, "did a large and satisfactory business," and visitors were "favorably impressed with the bargains offered." A "Mr. DeSpain," who resided on the E.V. Magill Ranch four miles west of Burnet, won the car. He immediately sold it to Mr. Ben Shaw, a former

Bluffton resident who had moved to Lampasas County.

The year ended with ads from The Wingren Company, Churchill Hardware and several others, wishing readers health, prosperity and joy in 1932.

CHAPTER FIVE

Burnet in 1932

The first issue of the *Burnet Bulletin* in 1932 acknowledged America's deepening depression but attempted to "emphasize the positive" in an article headlined, "Improvements Continue in Burnet." It pointed out that "notwithstanding the depression," there had been more new buildings in 1931 than in any year "since the railroad's advent some fifty years ago," and added the fact that more were on the way. It opined that "if conditions get back to normal this year, this town is going to blossom like a rose."

Another article that week reported that "engineers of the State Highway Commission have been surveying and blazing the route for the rebuilding of Highway No. 29, and actual construction will no doubt begin at an early date."

Dr. F.M. Johnson placed an ad to announce that he was moving his dental office "to the Frazier Building, over Leonard Wimpy's store." He promised "best work at cheaper prices," and expressed his willingness to barter "sheep, goats, calves, chickens, pigs and wood in exchange for dental work."

On January 14, the *Bulletin* reported that "work at Hamilton Dam is coming on at a fair rate of speed, with a goodly number of men on the job," and expressed the hope that "many more" would be hired as the weather improved.

But another article admitted that business was not good at the Burn-Tex Theatre (where Herman Schnabel had recently installed "the very latest talking picture" equipment), and urged residents to "go to the picture show."

The State Highway Commission appropriated $12,000 to "gravel Highway No. 66 to the Blanco County line, thus making it an all-weather road." The news story reported that "the road from Burnet to Marble Falls is fine except in wet weather, when it gets very slick and difficult to navigate in places." Money had also been appropriated to improve Hwy 29 from Austin to Liberty Hill.

On January 21, a front-page story reported that city officials had purchased a fire truck with a 350-gallon tank. It could pump water from a well or a cistern while hosing down a fire. The truck's list price was $2,800, but Burnet was able to buy a demonstrator for just $1,100 ($900 from the city, and $200 from the county). The formation of a volunteer fire company and the purchase of the truck would result in a 3% reduction in insurance rates in Burnet.

The Burnet Cream & Produce Co. announced that it would install "one of the latest electric model incubators" to do "custom hatching" and offer baby chicks for sale. Wimpy Grocery announced that it was opening a coffee shop "in connection with our grocery store," and invited everyone to come and see. The Burn-Tex Theatre advertised the Marx Brothers movie, "Monkey Business," for the last weekend in January.

A small item on February 4 announced big news; the Burnet National Bank had closed, and had been "placed in the hands of the Comptroller of the Currency." The article blamed "continued withdrawals and the inability to obtain the necessary financial assistance," but made it plain that trouble had been brewing at least since the closing of the Guthrie-Howell department store the previous February. Among the major shareholders in the bank were Dr. A. Howell, Eliza Guthrie and *Bulletin* publisher L.C. Chamberlain.

The next week's paper told of two burglaries in Burnet County. The first was at the Burnet Mercantile Store, between 4 and 5 a.m. on February 7 (according to night watchman Jake Clements, who said "everything appeared all right" when he made his rounds just before 4). An hour later, he discovered the burglary, which the *Bulletin* described as "the first burglary in Burnet in a long time." The burglars were unable to open the cash register, but escaped with about $300 in merchandise.

The second burglary was at the Fairland post office, one night after the Burnet burglary, when someone broke in and stole $19.14 in cash. Sheriff Ray arrested a 17-year-old boy the next day, who confessed and showed him where he had hidden the money. It took nearly two weeks and 1,300 miles of driving to track down three burglars from the first case. With help from store manager L.C. Clark, Sheriff Ray apprehended three men and recovered most of the stolen merchandise in Baylor County (near Wichita Falls). Sheriff Ray charged the county $4 in extra expenses related to that case!

Back then, $4 went quite a long way (literally and figuratively). An ad in the February 18 paper offered a Ford tune-up for $4.95. For that sum, Smith-Lloyd Motor Co. would "grind valves, clean carbon, tune motor, adjust distributor points, clean and adjust carburetor and spark plugs, adjust and re-set timing of ignition, clean gas lines, focus headlights, adjust fan, check battery and re-fill with distilled water."

Thomas C. Ferguson announced that he was running for re-election as representative of the 84th district (Burnet and Williamson Counties). The *Bulletin* praised him as "one of the brightest and most capable young men in this section of the state."

On March 3, the *Bulletin* reported that 1932 had (so far) "been the mildest and wettest winter" in memory. But, in the writer's words, "the depression goes merrily on. We are so used to being depressed that it has gotten to be a habit."

A week later, the weather had changed dramatically. Heavy rains and flooding, a "terrific wind" with "a great deal of thunder and lightning" preceded a hard freeze on March 5 and "by far the most severe weather of the winter" on March 8, when the temperature went down to 20 degrees. The next week's paper reported "there was ice" over most of the state for 10 consecutive days from March 5 to March 14 (including snowstorms as far south as Houston).

The American Society of Civil Engineers was planning its annual convention for April 15 and 16 in Austin, and a trip to the Hamilton Dam was on the group's agenda.

The Burnet County Commissioners Court raised the sheriff's salary to $1,000 per year, the legal limit for counties of its size, but Sheriff Ray announced that he would not run for re-election. That announcement triggered a flurry of candidacies, eventually reaching nine. It seemed to be a good-natured campaign; the nine candidates agreed to play Burnet's community baseball team in a charity game the next month!

On March 21, a "fearful sandstorm" swept into Burnet from the west, "at times almost reaching gale proportions."

In that Thursday's paper, Dickens Motor Co. advertised a special on "brake adjustments" for Chevrolets. The service would cost $1 for 1928 or 1929 model Chevrolets, but just 50 cents for the most recent three years' models.

The Presbyterian Church began construction on a 14' x 44' addition on the east side of its building, allowing for four new Sunday School classrooms when the folding doors were closed.

The Smith-Lloyd Motor Co. announced that the "beautiful new Ford car" would be on display in their showroom from 2:30 to 10 p.m. on April 13. The public was invited to inspect it.

Adam R. Johnson Jr. (son of the famous general), who had grown up in Burnet but was currently the city manager in Austin, presided over a meeting of Burnet businessmen "to discuss plans for a water works system for Burnet." He told the group that, although he now lived in Austin, Burnet was "the dearest place on earth" to him, and that he felt the town would greatly benefit from a water works. Mr. M.V. Smith (of Smith-Lloyd Motor Co.), who had recently come to Burnet from Taylor, described the benefits that a water works had provided for that town.

A "48 Years Ago" article told how General Adam R. Johnson had sold his "old English-looking home west of the creek" to "Mr. Badger" in 1884, and was building a "handsome rock residence on the commanding slope east of town" for a reported $7,500. (Editor's note: The two homes, now known as "Rocky Rest" and "Airy Mount" remain as historic treasures in Burnet in 2020).

A "very destructive fire" struck Burnet's King Cedar Yard, burning "more than 100 cars of cedar." The Burnet VFD and "other citizens" fought the flames for hours, preventing the fire from spreading. Owner F.W. King, of Austin, pledged to be back open for business "without delay."

W.E. Marx ("across from the Burnet Hotel") promised to fix anything that needed fixing, including "watches, clocks, spects, rings, portibles, pistols, guns, galvanized tanks, plumbing, flues and gutters." He also had a "motor grinder" for axes and tools.

Tom Huddleston, who had "nine years of experience in the professional dance business" and good connections with "the very best of jazz bands," leased the old Lone Star Theatre building and announced that he would "improve the condition of the building" for weekly Saturday night dances with big-name bands. The "well-known Burney Stinson Orchestra" would perform at the first dance, scheduled for April 23.

Gordon Fry was building a 9-hole golf course "on the old T.A. Chamberlain place in the southwestern part of town." While the writer of the article claimed to know "as much about golf as a cow knows about the ten commandments," he predicted success for the venture.

The worst possible news came on April 28. The front-page headline said, "Hamilton Dam work closed last Wednesday night," and the story mostly reflected on the benefits Burnet and Llano Counties had enjoyed because of the project. There was no news about any re-opening, but the *Bulletin* assured its readers that the dam was "sure to be completed sooner or later," and closed by saying, "This is no time to falter."

The next week's paper featured a re-printed article from the *San Antonio Express*, titled, "$6,000,000 Dam in Receivership." That story reported that Fargo Engineering Company, a creditor of Emery, Peck and Rockwood, had asked the Federal court to appoint a "receiver" to safeguard the assets of the company, which was "solvent, but unable to pay its obligations." State Senator Alvin J. Wirtz, of Seguin, was chosen for the job. He stated that the dam was "50 percent complete" and that the "administrative organization" would remain intact.

In what seemed like another sign of hard times, the Burnet Meat Market offered "choice meats" in the Burn-Tex Theatre building.

But not all the news was bad. Jim Tarver and Upton Fraser advertised a "new Ice House" (to be called "Jim-Up Ice Company") just "north of the Ideal Sandwich Shop" in that same week's paper.

Ray Summerow, who had been involved in the dam-building process since the beginning, was named General Manager of Hamilton Dam, and the *Bulletin* considered that a very good sign for the dam's future.

A May 12 item assured readers that work on the dam would re-sume "sooner or later," and opined that Burnet was "perhaps in better condition than 99 towns in every hundred in Texas." It urged citizens not to give up, and said, "Keep on trying and you will win!"

The Ideal Sandwich Shop ("North of Magnolia Filling Station") advertised "Day and Night Service," and urged readers to "Visit Us When Hungry." In addition to sandwiches, the shop offered "chili, oysters, pies, cakes, bottle drinks, cigars and candies."

There was more good news on May 19. A story told how "a num-ber of trucks for the past several days have been engaged in topping No. 66 between this place and Marble Falls." Several locals were working on that job.

Probably the best news of that difficult year came on May 26, when the *Bulletin* announced that Dr. J.L. Williamson had donated a huge, only-partly-explored cave and 500 surrounding acres to the State Park Board. No development plans had been announced, but the *Bulletin* believed that "eventually the park board will be joined by Burnet County in a program of improvements."

On June 2, Mrs. J.H. Guthrie's Shoppe advertised its entire stock at amazing prices. "All profit is forgotten," the ad said. "Cost is not even considered. Our only thought is to close out our entire stock as quickly as possible."

Possibly even sadder was a personal ad from Publisher L.C. Chamberlain. It said: "For Sale: My home in the eastern part of Bur-net, consisting of eight large rooms, pantry, bath, large sleeping porch galleries, never-failing water well, with running water over yard and in house, large underground cistern, stone and glass flower house, two-story well-house, garage, barn, cement reservoir, nine acres of land, two acres in cultivation, orchard and other improvements. In order to get the money to pay my assessment as a stock-holder in the Burnet National Bank, I will sell this house for two thousand dollars less than it has ever been held for. Anyone that ever intends to buy a sure enough home in Burnet should not fail to see me."

On June 9, the Austin & Northwest Railroad from Austin to Burnet was sold at a tax auction for $150,000. On June 23, an ad proclaimed that the Lone Star Picture Show would re-open, with D.F. Riggs as manager. On June 30, Raymond Coe (who had been working at the dam) was taking over "the Magnolia business for this section."

A benefit for the Burnet VFD was planned for July 9, with a "Vaudeville Show," a "thrilling play," and "special music" at the Burn-Tex Theatre. Admission would be a quarter for adults and a dime for children.

Chairman D.E. Colp, of the Texas State Parks Board, inspected the "gigantic cavern on state property in Burnet County," and gave a very optimistic report. He envisioned an underground theatre and eight miles of explorable passageways that would "rival any other cavern on this continent." He hoped to have it ready for visitors before the Texas Centennial in 1936, and expected many thousands of visitors that year.

This photo shows *Burnet Bulletin* publisher Louis Coleman "L.C." Chamberlain, with his wife Mary Alma in front of their home (located behind the David G. Burnet Hotel), probably in the early 1940s. They were leading citizens in Burnet for decades, and invested in several local businesses. The depression made 1932 a very stressful year for them.

Photo courtesy of Karl Piehl

The "Rainbow Sandwich Garden," on the grounds of the Burnet Hotel, offered a "couples" special: a toasted sandwich, pecan pie and a choice of coffee or iced tea (for both!) at just 20 cents.

On July 11, a well-attended Chamber of Commerce meeting discussed the possibilities of Longhorn Cavern. Another topic at the meeting was electric bills; the Chamber entreated business owners to keep the awning lights on at night, not only for looks, but as a deterrent to burglars. In return, the chamber promised to "confer with officials at Texas Power & Light" about lowering electric bills to "correspond with lowered prices of other commodities."

Mr. Lee Simmons, manager of the Texas Prison System, came to Longhorn Cavern on July 13 to "establish a camp where state convicts will be brought to make the improvements" at the cave. He assured concerned citizens in Burnet that "only the better type of convicts would be engaged in the work."

Another article in the July 14 paper commented that the cavern had been "known for almost half a century as Sherrard's Cave," but was "temporarily being called Longhorn Cave." It speculated that a contest would be held to decide the permanent name of the new state park.

That night (July 14), a fire broke out in the ice house at the Burnet Cream & Produce Co., and except for the "prompt and efficient work by the Burnet Volunteer Fire Department," it could have become a major disaster.

A plot of one hundred acres at "the Longhorn cave" was dedicated to the Texas Federation of Garden Clubs, who were to turn it into a beautiful garden all around the cave's entrance. An enthusiastic party of club leaders toured the site on August 13.

On August 18, the *Bulletin* reported that "the first contingent of convicts from the state penitentiary in Huntsville" passed through Burnet on Monday afternoon on their way to the Longhorn Cave, where they would begin cleaning out the cave for future visitors. This was the first of several groups of convicts who would arrive each week "until a great number of the laborers are on the grounds."

C.A. Baker was appointed to supervise work on Highway No. 66 going north from Burnet, and he announced that "fifteen or twenty men" would begin clearing right-of-way on Monday, August 29. He expected that 300 or 400 would eventually be employed on the project.

Will Everett, from eastern Burnet County, turned in the first bale of cotton on August 26, and in addition to the purchase price received premiums averaging almost a dollar in value from 39 Burnet businesses (including a $1.50 subscription to the *Bulletin*).

White Kitchen placed an ad on September 1, announcing that "Happy School Days are Here Again!" and offering deals on lunches and school supplies (plus a "little souvenir" for each student who stopped in).

One of the convicts at work on "Longhorn Cave" escaped on September 6, and was still at large at press time on September 8. The article mentioned that the project superintendent had moved his family to Burnet, and was residing in "one of the Guthrie residences on North Main Street."

Another article that week mentioned a story in "Texas Outlook" which claimed that Longhorn was the third-largest cave in the world, and (because it had not been completely explored) might end up being the largest in the world!

This photo shows Faye Chamberlain, daughter of L.C. and Mary Alma Chamberlain, standing in front of the entrance to Longhorn Cavern sometime in the early 1930s.

The iconic rock staircase used by modern tourists was built by the "CCC Boys" a few years later.

Photo courtesy of Karl Piehl

H.A. Barnett bested the other eight candidates in the Democratic primary for sheriff, and Sheriff Andy Ray (who had never been opposed in any of his three elections) resigned ahead of schedule, turning the job over to Mr. Barnett before the general election had been held. There was no Republican running.

School began on September 12 under new superintendent R.D. Williams. There were 100 students enrolled in the high school and

181 in the elementary school. An editorial recalled the days when Burnet's schools were some of the best in Texas, but lamented that "in recent years, the school has not maintained the standard."

A sad advertisement began appearing on September 15. It was titled, "The *Bulletin* and the Depression," and it explained that many newspapers had downsized as ad revenue fell between 1929 and 1932. The *Bulletin* had actually increased its size during that period, but had not raised its rates (and in fact, had not tried to collect from subscribers who had fallen behind). By September of 1932, the Bulletin was in need of cash to stay in business, and sent out a plea to all subscribers to pay $1.50 for the next year's subscription.

A September 29 article titled, "Waiting for the Right-of-Way" noted that the state had appropriated money for Highway No. 66 from Burnet to Lampasas, but work was apparently being held up by landowners who did not want to sell their property. The article ended by saying, "it is hoped that such will be secured with the least delay possible in order to give people work, if for no other reason."

On October 13, Neuman Bros. announced that its Burnet store would close. A special "Quitting Business" sale offered men's dress shirts for 39 cents and ladies' dresses for 49 cents. Boys' "aviator caps" with goggles cost only 29 cents.

The David G. Burnet Hotel, which had been thriving while work continued at the dam, began advertising new low prices. Rooms were offered for $1 to $2; meals were just 50 cents. The "new, modern" hotel advertised running water throughout, hot and cold baths, Beauty Rest mattresses and special rates for weekly or monthly stays.

An October 20 story announced that the general office of the Texas State Parks Board "is now located in Burnet," and that Chairman D.E. Colps "is now spending all his time in this section" as the opening of Longhorn Cave drew nearer. The formal opening of the cave was set for Thanksgiving weekend, and thousands of visitors were expected from around the state.

A new state law required all "wagons and trucks used on the highways after night to be equipped with lights or reflectors." Several accidents had been reported with farmers "going and returning from gins early and late at night."

Impressive progress was reported in "clearing up and otherwise beautifying the interior of Longhorn Cave" and making it "easier to explore the great cavern." Mr. D.E. Colps expected that "Longhorn Cave, when the improvement program is completed, will bring more money to Burnet County each year than all its cattle, sheep and goats combined."

A program for the cavern's official opening was published in the Bulletin on November 10. It would be four days of pageantry, beginning with a Thanksgiving service in the "Underground Cathedral" and continuing with speeches, meals, tours, music, dancing and more inside the cave, plus polo matches, rodeo events and other activities on the grounds.

The L.S. Chamberlain home on North Main Street, occupied at the time by Mr. and Mrs. Vernie Collins, burned completely to the ground after a gasoline cook stove exploded. The article noted that "this building was one of the old landmarks of Burnet, and was originally known as the Rawlings residence."

The John H. Olney Men's Store advertised bargains under the headline "We Must Have Money!" Offers included Wolverine Horse Hide Work Shoes for $3 and Good Grade Work Pants for just 59 cents.

The official opening at Longhorn Cave did not attract as big a crowd or as many dignitaries as hoped, but still the Bulletin reported "fair-sized crowds" each of the four days. Electric lighting had been added, and the story noted that it was "possible to travel almost two miles in comparative comfort." Ex-governor Pat Neff, who was then the president of Baylor University, was the keynote speaker.

By then, the Christmas season was in full swing, and Yarborough's Variety Store advertised its "Toy Town" with "Gifts for Everybody." Another ad said, "Laugh Off Your Worries! See Miss Blue Bonnet, a 3-act musical comedy at the Burn-Tex Theatre." And another offered "Depression Prices" ("school children 5 cents, outsiders 10 cents") for admission to a high school student program benefiting the football team.

The December 22 issue told how L.E. "Ed" Alexander had been reading the Bulletin regularly since its very first issue "59 years ago." His father was one of the original subscribers, and Ed got a subscription of his own when he got married.

A Red Cross benefit, including "Dominos, 42 and Bridge" plus "entertainment" was scheduled for Tuesday night, December 22.

The price of admission was "something to eat or wear."

An Old-Time Dance was planned for December 29 at the Lone Star Opera house to benefit the Burnet Fire Department.

The last issue of 1932 included "best wishes" ads from a good number of Burnet businesses. Among others, the Norris Shoe Shop, Humble Service Station, Riggs Barber Shop and Hokus Pokus thanked their customers and wished them happiness, health, prosperity and success in 1933.

CHAPTER SIX

Burnet in 1933

It was not an especially happy new year in Burnet in 1933, but there were a few bright spots in the news. Longhorn Cavern State Park was one of them; a film crew from Paramount Pictures, with all the latest in sound equipment, came to the cave for a weekend of filming at the beginning of January. The story in the *Burnet Bulletin* noted that a Friday night dance in the "Subterranean Ballroom" would be filmed, as would cavern guides in cowboy gear who planned to ride horses down into the Grand Foyer, several hundred feet underground. The story mentioned that eight miles of underground passageways had already been explored, and that many more were still unexplored.

But the really big issue in 1933 was the still-deepening Depression. A front-page ad on January 5 pleaded, "Pay your $1.50 (for readers' subscriptions) Now!" It continued, "The hard times make it impossible for us to continue sending the paper longer until it is paid," but offered to start the new subscription in 1934, thereby giving the customer a free year's subscription as an incentive to come up with the cash. The *Bulletin* also advertised its printing services, and offered to take payment "in trade."

A reprinted article from the *San Saba Star* made the front page on January 12. It described progress at Longhorn Cavern, mentioning that "much of the development is still underway, and it will be a much more interesting trip after the cavern has been more thoroughly developed." It mentioned that "experimental" lighting was in place, "but guides carry flashlights and brightly lighted lanterns to point out the various structures," and said, "Much work has been accomplished in building a road from the main highway and in excavating the passages in the cavern." It described an "array of tent concessions, resembling a gypsy camp" outside of the cavern entrance.

Olney's Men's Store advertised work pants, overalls and shirts on sale for just 59 cents apiece. Burnet Cream & Produce advertised "custom hatching and baby chicks for sale" at its new hatchery. The Burnet Fire Department advertised two "Old Time Dances" in February, and J.H. Stapp Jr. placed an ad complaining that he had loaned so many tools that he didn't have enough left to do his job. He asked friends to return the tools they had borrowed.

The Burnet Chamber of Commerce voted unanimously to resume its once-popular Trades Day, which had been discontinued as the Great Depression arrived in Texas a couple of years before. Members decided to offer cash prizes to attract customers from around the county. The first 1933 Trades day was scheduled for March 4.

In the meantime, things seemed to be getting worse. In a series of editorials, the normally mild-mannered publisher (L.C. Chamberlain) mentioned reports of farmers in the Northwest who banded together to prevent neighboring farms from being sold to pay back taxes, and lamented the fact that government was costing 20 percent of Americans' meager income. In one especially forceful article, he wrote, "The great rank and file of the people are breaking under the burden they are forced to carry, and mutterings are heard on every hand. You'd better get busy, Mr. Legislator! The slumbering volcano is liable to erupt most any time." He ended by saying, "This isn't idle talk; it's the stark, naked truth . . . CONDITIONS CANNOT STAY AS THEY ARE FOR ANOTHER TWELVE MONTHS!"

By the end of February, the tone of the editorial was slightly more upbeat; the headline said, "Burnet has a Future," and one of the main points made was that too much money had already been spent on the Hamilton Dam to just abandon the project. "It is true that the dam work is suspended," Mr. Chamberlain wrote, "but it will start again some time without any doubt at all."

The local American Legion and Auxiliary announced a joint

meeting at their hall for March 2. Mr. and Mrs. M.J. Bennefield would be there from Brady to "complete the organization of the local Unit," and "wives, mothers, sisters and daughters of Legionnaires or of deceased veterans of the World War" were invited to join the Auxiliary.

Large portraits of president-elect Franklin D. Roosevelt and his running mate, John Nance Garner, adorned the front page of the *Bulletin* on the Thursday after FDR's inauguration (March 4, 1933), and his bold new program (along with his famous declaration that "We have nothing to fear but fear itself!") drowned out the news of a successful Trades Day that same day. It also seemed to give new hope to Burnet County. Among the immediate measures was a national "bank holiday" to stop the rush to withdraw money while programs to instill confidence in the banking system were enacted (FDIC, etc.)

The very next week, more than forty local businesses and leading citizens joined in a large ad congratulating the First State Bank of Burnet on being "among the first of the banks in the smaller towns of Texas" to re-open after the "holiday." An accompanying article explained that only banks which had been "recognized as perfectly safe and sound" were allowed to open so soon.

Another Trades Day was announced for Saturday, April 1, and an ad promised "Big Times! Big Bargains!" The *Bulletin* was much more optimistic in its outlook by the end of March, but cautioned readers, "Do not Expect Too Much!" from President Roosevelt, who would require steadfast support in the coming months to "get things on an even keel."

"Topping Highway No. 66" was the subject of an article that week, and the *Bulletin* expected that "when this work is completed, a better highway will be hard to find in this state."

J.H. Stapp Jr. was making some major improvements on his Hanford-Stapp building, occupied in 1933 by Neuman's Dry Goods Store. "A new front with attractive show windows" would be installed along with other changes to improve looks and convenience for customers.

W.C. Galloway announced that he would run for a second term as Burnet's mayor. President Roosevelt made the news by eating a seven-and-one-half-cent meal, prepared by the home economics department of Cornell University, and pronouncing it "good."

A small news item that week declared that "thinking people in Europe fear that they are on the brink of another bloody war, which is likely to involve every major nation in the Old World. It is not likely that the United States will be drawn into the conflict."

On April 6, the Burnet Fire Department invited residents to a dance that evening at the Lone Star Theatre, and promised "red hot music." Kenneth Williamson offered to rebuild electric irons for just 75 cents, and added "I can fix any electric appliance and save you money."

A news item reported that the fire department's second truck was now ready for service, and that it would "double the amount of water with which to fight fires."

A large front-page ad that week announced Opening Day for Granite League baseball, with the Burnet team at home, facing off against Kingsland at 3 p.m. on Sunday, April 9. A partially legible box score in the following week's paper indicated that Burnet had won the game 19-8.

Thomas C. Ferguson, "one of the brightest young men this place has ever produced," was appointed as a member of the Democratic State Executive Committee. He was a self-taught lawyer who passed the bar exam "with high honors" and was elected to the state legislature at age 23!

The Executive Committee of the American Association of State Highway Officials designated the partially completed Hwy No. 66 in Texas to become part of U.S. Highway 281, which would run (as a paved highway) from Canada to Mexico. Work to fill in gaps in Blanco and Burnet Counties would go to the top of the Highway Department's priority list.

Robert Wagner began building "a double-deck ice cream stand" on the lot adjoining the Burnet Hotel. A "Baseball Dance" was scheduled (at an undisclosed location) for Thursday night, May 4. There would be "both modern and ole time music," and the "entire proceeds" would go to the baseball team.

Descendants of "Dr. and Mrs. Moore, early settlers of Burnet," held a family reunion at the Burnet Hotel, which included at least three sons and one daughter of the couple. Old-time friend Captain T.E. Hammond took them on a tour of Longhorn Cavern, and the whole group (about 35) paid a visit to the *Bulletin* office (which they said their ancestor had built!)

A highlight of the Burnet Chamber's May meeting was the announcement by Thomas C. Ferguson that Houghton Brownlee intended to host a huge BBQ at his ranch on July 4th. The festivities would include exhibition races by some of his famous horses and speeches by political celebrities.

On May 18, an upbeat editorial claimed that "there is no doubt at all that conditions are improving along almost every line of endeavor. The prices of all farm and ranch commodities are considerably higher."

The Texas State Legislature raised the age for starting "free school" from six to seven. A story about the 1933 "commencement exercises" said, "Under the able superintendency of Mr. Williams, the school has progressed during the past year in a very satisfactory manner indeed."

A special meeting of the "Ira J. Dawson Camp" of Spanish-American War Veterans was held in Burnet on May 12, with dignitaries from around Texas in attendance.

A May 25 story titled, "Great Improvements at Longhorn Cavern," told how iron railings and gates had been installed around the entrance, and the ballroom floor had been enlarged. It said, "good progress has been made in cleaning out the debris in various parts of the cavern" and added that "a big dance will be held in the ball room Saturday night." Music would be provided by the Harris Brothers "Texans," a Brunswick Recording Orchestra, and a "big-town floor show" would feature a "torch singer" and a dancer "with a chorus of beautiful girls." The event would be broadcast live on WOAI Radio in San Antonio.

Saturday, May 27, was designated as Poppy Day, and the American Legion Auxiliary had "Veteran Made" crepe paper poppies for sale to support disabled veterans.

Robert Wagner announced plans for a new ice factory across the street from the Burnet Hotel. He would begin with a five-ton capacity, which could be increased as demand dictated.

Twenty-one Burnet County boys were sent to Camp Bullis to begin training for President Roosevelt's new Forestry Conservation unit, which would send them wherever they were needed in the western half of the country.

A Ford ad was published in the form of a personal letter from founder Henry Ford, in which he called himself the "first Ford Dealer" and told how he had built, sold and even delivered Ford cars in the early days of his business. He said that country doctors were the first to recognize the benefits of his economical, dependable cars, and that he still heard from some of them more than 30 years later. He closed by saying that the 1933 Ford was the best ever, with its "powerful and smooth-running" V-8. He called the car "very good looking" with "comfortable riding qualities," and "the fastest, roomiest and most powerful car we have ever built."

The June 6 paper reported that work had been resumed on the 12-mile stretch of Highway No. 66 still needed to complete the highway from Burnet north to the Lampasas County line. Another article reported that the Burnet Fire Department had extinguished two fires on the previous Wednesday evening: one at Dump Norred's house and another in Hubert Dickens' barn.

Mr. A.W. Elrod, of the Texas Rehabilitation and Relief Commission, told a group of Burnet businessmen how President Roosevelt's "vast public works program" could help the area, calling it an "ungloved knockout punch" at the Depression. The program would include construction of many public buildings, roads and infrastructure projects.

But the Depression was by no means finished, and an ad in that week's paper showed Uncle Sam addressing cotton growers. "There is a 13 million bale surplus. Reduce crop NOW to prevent trouble later. It's up to YOU!"

County Agent A.J. Cotton held "one of the largest mass meetings ever held in Burnet" the following week to organize farmers for the "cotton relief program." Farmers would be partially compensated for "retiring" some of their acreage, but there were strict rules about how the "retired" land could be used. Growers were asked to fill out forms to offer from 25 to 50 percent of their land.

Another Trades Day was announced for July 1. Merchants invited the public to enjoy "Special Prices and Other Attractions." Parks Cash Grocery announced its informal opening that day, with "Iced Beverage Served Free Throughout the Day."

As June came to a close, the *Bulletin* noted that the "extremely hot dry weather of the past few days has about put the finishing touches on the corn crop" in most parts of the county. It also mentioned that local cotton crops "also needed rain."

Hot weather notwithstanding, Burnet County farmers finally had some hope that things were getting better. The *Bulletin* opined in July that "perhaps never within the history of this government has any president held the confidence of the rank and file of the people to the degree that President Roosevelt has." The editorial continued, "Conditions are steadily and in many instances rapidly improving. We are still not out of the woods, but every one thinks he can see the light ahead, and President Roosevelt is getting the credit."

And G. Schlomach brought some fine ears of corn (grown by his son, William) to the *Bulletin* office, saying that he had not expected much of a crop, but perhaps due to cool nights and a dry spring which caused the roots to grow deeper than usual to reach moisture, the corn crop was as good as ever.

An unnamed citizen brought a plan to the *Bulletin* office, recommending that a small dam be built "across Hamilton Creek near the Mrs. Mary Gibbs property" to create a little lake for swimming and fishing. He suggested a small admission charge to cover expenses.

Parks Cash Grocery ("next door to the post office") thanked customers for "the splendid support we have received," and urged them to "watch our windows for week-end specials."

The eagerly anticipated "free barbecue" at Houghton Brownlee's ranch was rescheduled for Saturday, July 22. Guests of honor included the 143rd Infantry Band.

County Agent A.J. Cotton announced that 913 farmers had "offered for retirement 12,827 acres," but urged them not to begin destroying cotton until they were officially notified that their offers had been accepted.

Herman Pogue brought in Burnet County's first bale of cotton, grown on J.H. Guthrie's Gabriel farm, on Thursday, August 3. Mr. Pogue received "close to $40" in premiums from local businesses.

Bill Foster announced that he was opening an ice house "in the building lately occupied by W.J. Tarver." W.J. Tarver ("Ice & Produce") announced a "New Location" between Biggs' Market and Craddock's Texaco Station. Parks Cash Grocery announced that two sacks of Gold Medal Flour would be given away at 3 p.m. on Saturday, August 5.

Vice President John Nance Garner made front-page news at the end of August by calling for the repeal of the 18th Amendment to the U.S. Constitution, saying that prohibition had not "produced a satis-factory or effective solution to the temperance problem."

In early September, local business owners held a meeting to orga-nize a committee to "carry on President Roosevelt's National Recov-ery Act" in Burnet County. The Young People's class of the Methodist Sunday School sponsored a "Mexican Supper and Program" at the Lone Star Opera House on Friday, September 8. Tickets were avail-able (for 35 cents) at Guthrie Drug or Burnet Mercantile.

Burnet's schools opened on Monday, September 11, and a crowd of interested citizens was "on hand to witness the beginning of oper-ations." Enrollment in the high school rose by four from the previous year (to 116 total) and in the elementary, there was "a large increase" to 198 total pupils.

On September 19, the City of Burnet applied for a grant and loan package totaling $53,239 from the Public Works Administration to build a municipal water system.

On September 21, the *Bulletin* reported a "Record Dry Spell" in and around Burnet, saying, "wells in town that had supplied an abundance of water for many years have gone dry, and all kinds of vegetation has withered."

In a shocking cost-cutting move, the county commissioners court voted to "discontinue the services" of County Agent A.J. Cotton after January 1, 1934. The *Bulletin* reported that an immediate effort had begun to make sure that Mr. Cotton's services were retained, and ex-pressed its opinion that he had proven to be "worth a great deal more to the people of Burnet County" than the small salary he had been paid.

The county agent continued to do his job, and every week's paper contained some kind of message to the county's farmers. On Sep-tember 28, he relayed a message from the Secretary of Agriculture, clarifying the rules on the allowable uses for "retired" acreage: crops planted solely for soil-improvement or erosion-prevention were en-couraged. Gardens for personal use were allowed, provided that they did not free up other land for cash crops.

On October 5, the *Bulletin* published an editorial suggesting that the cotton-reduction program alone had resulted in a $70,000 benefit to Burnet County, which would not have been possible without the services of a County Agent.

Also that week, county relief administrator Fred Craddock announced that there would "soon be a limited number of vacancies in the Civilian Conservation Corps" to be filled for six-month terms by unmarried young men (aged 18-25) from Burnet County. Each "CCC Boy" would be paid $30 per month on condition that $20-25 be sent home to their families.

The Burnet Hotel announced its new Rainbow Coffee Shop, which offered "a large variety of delicious food" plus "real coffee," made in "an electric Drip-O-Later." And the Greathouse cotton gin announced that it would "pay top market price" for turkeys.

On November 16, the *Bulletin* announced that Fred Craddock was now the "Civil Works Administrator" for Burnet County, and that (instead of distributing cash or food to those in need) he would be offering jobs to unemployed residents. The plan was to immediately hire 208 workers for 30 hours per week at 40 cents per hour on projects which would benefit the public.

A big front-page ad that week announced a football game "at High School Field" between Burnet and Marble Falls.

The Rainbow Coffee Shop offered a new "Pit-Barbecued Beef Sandwich" ("First Time Ever Served in Burnet!"). Other menu highlights were oysters and "good coffee."

Burnet County's Civil Works Program announced that it had begun operations with 281 employees (84 in Burnet).

The Agricultural Adjustment Administration announced a plan to buy a limited number of hogs at above-market prices to help farmers who could not afford to either feed or sell them.

An article from Marble Falls bragged that "Texas Pink Granite" was selling all across the country. "More than 1,000 carloads are being shipped at present to a project at Texas City. Shipments are shortly to go to Los Angeles for the new building of the Los Angeles Times, to New York for Columbia University and to Houston for the $1,500,000 passenger station of the Southern Pacific."

A December 7 article announced that the Highway Department was accepting bids for construction of 7.816 miles of Hwy No. 66 in northern Burnet County, and that jobs would soon be available. Skilled laborers would earn 45 cents per hour, and unskilled laborers would make 35 cents per hour. Skilled carpenters and ironworkers could earn as much as 75 cents.

Willis Smith, who had worked for 28 years at the same business (Badger-King, Badger-Johnson, Guthrie-Howell and finally Burnet Mercantile), had purchased the company's inventory and would be operating as W.H. Smith. The *Bulletin* noted that "this is the consummation of an ambition that he cherished for many years," and wished him well in his new endeavor.

A front-page article in mid-December was titled, "Dry and Getting Dryer," and lamented the lack of rain since early in the spring. It said, "There will perhaps be more prickly pear fed in Burnet County this year than for many years past."

The *Bulletin* predicted that many Burnet County residents would be gainfully employed through the winter on the 8-mile section of Highway 66 that had been put out to bid, and that (when completed) the highway would bring much-increased traffic through Burnet County. It also applauded improvements by new manager Tommie White at the Burn-Tex Theatre and noted that manager Hob Galloway was expecting "large numbers of visitors" at Longhorn Cavern during the holiday season that year.

And there was even good news from the defunct Burnet National Bank, as the court-appointed receiver distributed a third dividend (making a total of 60 cents on the dollar) from the bank's assets.

At the end of this most trying year, the *Bulletin* looked back over the history of the north-south highway that bisected Burnet. It had been about fifteen years since the first meeting had been held with other communities on the projected route of the "Air Line" highway. The designation had been changed to Highway 108, then Highway 66, then U.S. Highway 281. By 1933, it was becoming one of the "most important (roads) in Texas."

An ad from Burnet County officials graced the final issue of 1933; it sent wishes for a "Happy and Prosperous 1934," from County Judge O.B. Zimmerman, County Clerk H.F. Atkinson, Sheriff H.A. Barnett, Tax Collector Cecil Humphries, Tax Assessor Vernon Greer and County Attorney H. Edward Johnson. That was the news in Burnet in 1933.

CHAPTER SEVEN

Burnet in 1934

Political announcements made front-page news on January 4, 1934. Even though the Democratic primary was still six months away, six candidates had already thrown their hats into the ring. James E. Box was challenging incumbent O.B. Zimmerman for the office of County Judge. Mrs. Dock Maxwell and Lucy Lamon both were challenging Mrs. J.M. Trotter for her position as County Treasurer, and W.T. Morris was running for re-election as County Commissioner for Precinct #2.

Fire alarms went off on New Year's Day and on January 2, and volunteer firefighters put out a car fire at Wilson's Filling Station (on the east side of town) and a grass fire "two or three miles north of town."

The First State Bank of Burnet met all the qualifications of the 1933 Glass-Stegall Act and became a member of the Federal Deposit Insurance Company, a step which the *Bulletin* believed would "re-establish confidence" of local patrons shaken by the disastrous closing of Burnet National Bank.

The *Bulletin* re-printed an article by editor John J. Faubion, of the *Marble Falls Messenger*, explaining the workings of the recently created Civil Works Administration (a Federal program which aimed to provide manual labor jobs for roughly one fourth of the millions who were unemployed at the time). Burnet County had "between 1,000 and 1,200" people looking for work, and the

CWA's quota for the county was 284. Fred Craddock, of Burnet, was the county administrator for the program, and his unenviable job was to choose which 284 people got the jobs. The article praised Mr. Craddock's efficiency and fairness, and emphasized that the county commissioners had no say whatsoever in who was hired.

A "birthday ball" was planned to celebrate President Roosevelt's 52nd birthday on January 30. The event would honor the president by raising funds to help fight "infantile paralysis," which had partially crippled FDR.

The *Bulletin* reported that week (January 18) that an "important real estate sale" had taken place. Mrs. Leonard Frazier had sold her "large farm and ranch just north of the city limits" to Mr. R.S. Bowden, who planned to move to the "splendid new modern home" from his former residence in Tobyville.

The Texas congressional delegation united to request $4 million of public works money for the completion of Hamilton Dam. Their request was helped considerably by the participation of Representative James P. Buchanan, who had been appointed as chairman of the House Appropriations Committee in 1933.

T.O. Whitaker announced that he would be leaving his employment with the Burnet Lumber Co. and opening his own lumber yard ("west of W.H. Smith's dry goods business"). The following week, an announcement that "Mr. Chester Hilbern, from Menard, has been in charge of the Burnet Lumber Co. business at this place for the past several days."

A re-printed story from the *Austin American* reported on February 15 that former city manager Adam R. Johnson Jr. (son of the famous general) had been appointed as Texas State Relief Director. Governor Miriam "Ma" Ferguson welcomed him to the job, calling him an "honest and efficient man." Another re-printed article noted that Austin had joined Burnet and Llano Counties in calling for the completion of Hamilton Dam; four "elements of interest" were listed in the article: flood control, water conservation, creation of a recreational lake which would also generate electric power, and creation of badly needed construction jobs.

The *Bulletin* reported almost a full week of rains, estimating that the total had been "five or six inches" in Bethel, and saying, "All streams are higher than they had been for years."

The Burnet Fire Department hired M.W. Nolan on March 12 to add a second floor to their one-story fire hall (so they could hold meetings without finding parking spots for their trucks outside the building); he started work on the project on March 14.

Administrator Fred Craddock sent a letter to the editor (published on March 15), announcing the "third enrollment for the Civilian Conservation Corps" sometime in April.

A joint meeting of citizens from Burnet and Bertram was held at the courthouse in mid-March to begin planning ways to "have Highway No. 29 straightened and improved from the Williamson County line on through Bertram to Burnet." The *Bulletin* reported that "quite a number from both towns" were in attendance.

A front-page story on March 29 reported that many freshly sheared goats had died from "cold, rainy weather" the previous week.

Robinson Bros. Bus Line announced "new low fares" from Burnet to Austin ($1.45 one way; $2.20 round trip). Buses left Burnet at 8:20 a.m. and 4 p.m. each day, and took about one hour and forty minutes to make the trip to Austin.

There was good news on April 5. Congressman J.P. Buchanan announced that he "had been given every assurance" that the public works administration would approve $4,500,000 for completion of the Hamilton Dam in the very near future.

The Wm. P. Carey Lumber Co. announced, "Lumber Prices Slashed to Bottom." It offered, among other products, "No. 1 Grade 6 ft. 2x4s" at "$3.80 per 100 Ft." and 2 gallons of "best grade" exterior paint for $3.98.

The Burnet Chamber of Commerce, which had "not been functioning for several months," was re-organized in April. Seven local leaders were chosen to form a board of directors; Roy Fry was elected president.

The April 25 *Bulletin* announced that the CCC camp, which would be in charge of improvements at Longhorn Cavern State Park, would be located in Marble Falls. The article noted that Burnet leaders had been "working for months" to have a camp located at the cavern, and still felt that was the best location.

A "Mr. P.A. Sullivan, with the state highway department," came to Burnet with his "Magnetic Nail Picker," which gathered all kinds of small metal objects from the highway, "no doubt saving the people of Texas many thousands of dollars" in tire damage.

Just two weeks later, the *Bulletin* published an article, reporting that the CCC Camp, which had been located in Blanco, had been moved to Longhorn Cavern the previous week, and the "CCC Boys" were busy setting up living quarters for a lengthy stay. Several CCC executives were planning to move their families to residences in Burnet. On May 24, the *Bulletin* published the first of a series of "Longhorn Cavern News" articles, furnished by the CCC Boys. That article told how "Company 854" had received orders to move to Longhorn Cavern the previous Wednesday, and twenty enrollees with three trucks full of supplies had been on their way within an hour. By that night, they had set up tents at the state park and begun to cut cedar for firewood. Several more truckloads arrived the next day!

The May 31 paper noted the FBI's recent killing of notorious criminals Clyde Barrow and Bonnie Parker the previous week, and cautioned readers not to waste "misplaced sympathy" on the murderous pair "even though one of them was a woman."

That week's paper also contained the news that a "large mess hall, recreation and headquarters building" had already been completed by the CCC Boys at Longhorn Cavern ("save for some finishing touches"). There was apparently already a rodeo field at the park, and a big ad that week invited the public to attend a formal opening of the park with two rodeo performances on Saturday and Sunday, June 9 and 10, by "Leonard Stroud's Congress of World Champion Cowboys and Cowgirls, recently from Madison Square Garden in New York."

The "CCC Chatter" column the following week reported that two of the CCC Boys had been injured, one quite severely, when a large rock had fallen on them in the cavern. Joe Treiber had been taken to the Station hospital in Fort Sam Houston by ambulance.

Another article reported that a road "through the Duncan pasture" from Hoover Valley Road had been completed, and travel to and from the cavern would be quicker and simpler in the future.

The "Longhorn Cavern News" section announced on June 16 that work was going well at the new state park, and that "rock has been quarried for the stone cabins" to be built there. Tourists were visiting in increasing numbers, and the geology class from Southwestern University was planning another trip through the cave to study rock formations.

Parks Cash Grocery advertised some interesting specials for June 22 and 23. A can of pork and beans was selling for a nickel, a box of corn flakes or a 5-pound sack of potatoes cost a dime and a quart of pure mustard cost 14 cents. Ford Motor Company advertised "112-inch wheelbase" passenger cars ranging in price from $505 for the Coupe "with standard equipment" to $615 for a Fordor Sedan "with De Luxe equipment." A 131-inch truck chassis cost $485, and a 157-inch stake truck with closed cab cost $715.

A big political rally was announced for July 21 in Burnet by Democratic County Chairman J.H. Guthrie. All "precinct, county, district and state candidates" were invited to "present their claims to the voters."

Hardware store owner W.F. LaForge had a narrow escape when he fell from a scaffold into a tool display and "the prong of a pitchfork passed entirely through his hand."

On July 5, the *Bulletin* featured a banner headline announcing, "PWA allots $4,500,000 to Complete Hamilton Dam." The front-page story noted that "It is doubtful if any announcement ever before made in Burnet caused such wide-spread and general rejoicing as was manifested by our people last Thursday evening when the above information was received."

Another (much smaller) item that week announced that a new cooling system had been installed in the Burn-Tex Theatre by "Mr. White."

On July 12, the Longhorn Cavern News reported a good crowd of visitors on July 4, with some bringing lunches and spending their whole day at the park. The new CCC Camp had "200 boys," and work was progressing well. They were removing dirt from the "Sam Bass entrance" and the Cathedral Room, sinking a shaft down to the Lake Room and building and improving the trail through the cave.

On July 26, another banner headline noted that the name of the half-built dam had been changed to "BUCHANAN DAM!" in honor of Congressman J.P. Buchanan "for his work in helping to secure government funds for the completion of the mighty structure." The story reported that Houghton Brownlee had suggested the name change during a regional meeting at the dam site the previous week, and that the motion was "enthusiastically seconded by citizens from every county along the Colorado River." The purpose of the meeting was to organize the "Colorado Valley Water Area Regional Planning Board."

A smaller article announced that L.C. Chamberlain, Bill Chamberlain and Ross Johnson had formed a new real estate business, with offices in the *Burnet Bulletin* building. Another article announced that Burnet would receive a combination loan and grant from the federal government for $46,000 to build a water works, another long-sought step forward for the little town.

But still another article that week was less upbeat. Burnet County's "drouth" had worsened, and the county had been advanced from "primary" to "emergency" status. Checks were reportedly on the way to help hard-hit ranchers pay for feed to keep their livestock alive. The government purchased 6,000 head of Burnet County cattle, killing "a little more than 50 percent" at the ranches and transporting the rest out of the county by train. At the same time, workers were moving fish from the "shallow holes" going dry on the Colorado River downstream from Marble Falls and releasing them above the dam where they would have a chance for survival.

A front-page article on August 16 was titled, "The Menace of the Drouth," and listed various dangers from the lack of rainfall. Perhaps most worrisome was that "here in Burnet, wells that withstood the drouth of last year are showing signs of failure, and it is feared their water supply will soon cease unless rain comes and in abundance."

But life went on, and another article that week noted that the S&H Construction Co. had completed its job on the seven miles of Highway 66 just north of Burnet. The *Bulletin* called it "the best looking dirt road anywhere in this section of Texas," but mentioned that there were "still twelve miles of this road to be built on through Burnet County to the Lampasas County line."

The Longhorn Cavern News that month reported that "the shaft that the boys have been digging from the top of the ground down into the lake room of the Cavern was completed," and would be used as a ventilator and a way to lift dirt out of that part of the cavern. It called that section "more beautiful than anything that is now open to visitors." It estimated that the additional section of accessible cave would mean "three hours to complete the trip through." Also, the fence around the park property was finished, and a foundation had been laid for the first of 15 stone tourist cabins. Six wood barracks buildings were to be built before winter to house the CCC Boys (40 in each building) who were doing the work.

On September 6, the Longhorn Cavern News reported that work had begun (by local carpenters) on the barracks buildings, and that the CCC Boys were making progress on a road from the park to Hwy 66. Management reported a flood of visitors the previous week; Houston residents were the most numerous, followed by good numbers from Dallas, Austin and Fort Worth.

Later that month, the *Bulletin* lamented the still-worsening drouth, and said, "It is not the depression, but the drouth, that is causing apprehension and anxiety in Burnet County." It called the "wide-spread drouth in almost every section of the United States" a "severe blow to President Roosevelt's New Deal," and opined that, without the drouth, "Texas would have been decidedly improved when compared with recent years."

State Relief Director Adam R. Johnson recommended "the sledge hammer and rock pile" for men who collected relief money and spent it on drink "instead of providing food and clothing for their families." He noted that "a large percentage of the drunks picked up from the streets are relief roll clients."

Near the end of September, the Texas Senate passed a bill creating the Colorado River Authority. The Texas House of Representatives killed the bill the very next week, citing objections by the West Texas Chamber of Commerce.

In the meantime, the Burnet Chamber of Commerce debated possible routes for the proposed upgrade of Hwy 29 through the city. Mayor W.C. Galloway advocated that the current route along Jackson Street should be preserved with just a few improvements, including the removal of a house belonging to "Mrs. Tumlinson."

Nearly $5 million was approved for a federal "emergency road construction" program in Central Texas, and the remaining 12 mile stretch of Hwy 66 to the Lampasas County line was one of the projects included. There was no firm timeline; the *Bulletin* expressed its hope that "the letting of the contract may not be long delayed."

At the end of October, local contractor M. Nolen started work on a "stucco store building on the property on the east side of the public square, owned by District Clerk Walter Wallace." The building-to-be had already been rented to H.F. Warden Jr., from Bertram, who

who planned to open a grocery business there.

The Longhorn Cavern News section on November 1 reported that Manager Hob Galloway had taken a Longhorn Cavern exhibit to the State Fair, and that his booth had attracted "more attention than any other in the building." Also, a geology professor from Texas A&M had been to the cavern and had announced plans to bring classes there every year. The CCC Boys were making good progress removing dirt from the cave, but reported that in some sections, they had to go down 20 feet to reach solid rock.

W.H. Smith announced in the beginning of November that he would be moving his dry goods business into the former Burnet National Bank building on the southeast corner of the square.

The Texas State Legislature came to an agreement, and both houses passed a bill to create the Colorado River Authority on November 10. The headline in the next week's *Bulletin* screamed, "Buchanan Dam Sure!"

Schnabel's Bakery and Grocery advertised "10 lbs. Spuds" for 19 cents, "10 pounds Cane Sugar" for $.50 and "2 Large 14 oz. Bottle Catsup" for a quarter.

A headline read, "Believe it or Not," and the story told how a rancher had been looking for hands to hire. He found only five young men in Burnet who wanted the jobs, and had to go elsewhere to get a full crew. The *Bulletin* remarked that "six or seven years ago, such an item would not have been classed as news," but considering the recent job situation, this was an exciting sign for the future.

Walter Wallace's new building was finished (on the east side of the square), and H.F. Warden had announced the opening of his new "Cash and Carry" grocery store on November 24. He had hired F.H. Rogers to help him manage the new business, and the *Bulletin* reported that both were "experienced in the grocery trade."

There was lots of news from Longhorn Cavern on November 29; another hoist had been installed over an opening into the cave, and there were now four motorized hoists which could lift huge buckets full of dirt and debris from the inside of the cave. A rock-crusher was busy providing material for trails inside the cave and roads outside. A carload of cement had arrived the previous week, and was being used to build culverts and bridges. Rapid progress was being made on the new limestone-and-cypress administration center, and the first cedar-and-native-stone tourist cabin was nearly finished. A good crowd of tourists was expected for Thanksgiving.

The "CCC Boys" work on the limestone-and-cypress Administration Building at Longhorn Cavern State Park during 1934 or 1935.

Photo courtesy of Texas Parks & Wildlife

A front-page story at the end of November announced, "The Drouth is Broken!" The barely legible story reported that, as of press time, rain had been falling "almost constantly at this place for the past eight hours."

The December 4 *Bulletin* announced that Dr. J. Odd Hamilton and his wife had returned to Burnet from El Paso, where they had purchased machinery for an ichthyol mill just north of town (editor's note: from what I see online, ichthyol is a controversial substance made from natural oil shale rock and used to treat skin diseases. It was quite popular in the early 1900s, and is still used by some people these days). The article reported that "a careful analysis of the (local) ichthyol rock has been made, which we understand has proven very satisfactory." The mill was expected to be operational in the near future.

Night watchman Jake Clements scared off some night prowlers at the Garrett Hotel (where the First State Bank of Burnet is now located, on the northeast corner of the square) by firing warning shots into the air, but not before they broke into several cars and stole some property. The prowlers sped off in a late-model "Chevrolet or Ford."

A "little cottage, adjoining the Sinclair Filling Station on Hwy 66" caught fire on a Tuesday afternoon, but quick action by volunteer firefighter Boxie Marx saved it from complete destruction. The interior of the building was damaged, and some furniture was ruined.

A December 20 article reported that the ichthyol mill was basically completed, but workers were still setting up the recently purchased machinery. The story continued, "it is the *Bulletin's* understanding that this is the only known ichthyol deposit in the U.S.," and "there are other valuable by-products in the rock," such as "paint pigments, dyes, insecticides, antiseptic, animal dips, flotation oils and dehydrated lime base for fertilizers."

Walter Wallace began construction on another new building just before Christmas, adjoining his still-new Cash and Carry grocery store building on the east side of the square. The *Bulletin* reported that "it was necessary to tear down the wooden building" on that lot, which had "been occupied by the Norris Shoe Shop for a long time" and, before that, by the late Ealy J. Moses as a land and abstract office. The Norris Shoe Shop had moved temporarily into a back room at the First State Bank building.

The last issue of the *Bulletin* for 1934 reported that Christmas had gone well, "with no disturbances at all," and that "various churches have put on nice Christmas entertainments." Singled out for special praise was the Burn-Tex Theatre, where owner Tommie White had presented a free picture show for all the children in town, accompanied by gifts of fruit and toys which had been donated by businesses and individuals around town.

And in another piece of good news, that week's paper reported that a contract had been awarded to Cage Bros. Construction for the completion of 11.84 miles on Hwy 66, the final section in northern Burnet County. Not only would this give Burnet County an excellent road, but it would provide employment to dozens of local men for the next several months.

CHAPTER EIGHT

Burnet in 1935

The new year began with an assessment of Burnet's condition and its prospects for 1935 on the front page of the *Burnet Bulletin* under the headline "What of 1935?" The first point made was that 1934 "made a record as the driest year ever known" but hastened to add that "people are perhaps feeling more hopeful than they have for several years." It commended FDR's administration for having "the welfare of its people at heart" and listed several ways that government programs had helped local farmers and ranchers, adding that things would have been much better without the widespread drought.

The article predicted that (assuming normal rainfall) "prosperity will in great measure return," and listed several reasons for that optimism. Construction on Hwy 66 was one reason, and another was the CCC Camp at Longhorn Cavern State Park, but "the greatest of all" was the projected resumption of work at Buchanan Dam in February. Another hoped-for project was the waterworks in Burnet; bids were set to be opened on January 11.

A report from "a recent Burnet County grand jury" gave very poor reviews to the current courthouse and jail, calling both buildings "a disgrace to the citizenry of the county," and noting that the federal government had offered a 30% grant and a 50-year loan toward the building of a new courthouse through its Public Works System.

Tommie White, who owned the Burn-Tex Theatre on the east side of the square, purchased property on the north side of the square, "consisting of the residence occupied by H.D. Crawford and his mother, and the rock building adjoining, in which Mr. Crawford has his law office. It also extends around the Garrett Hotel property and faces the Presbyterian church."

Louis Wagner began moving his stock of groceries (temporarily) from "the building between Dickens Motor Co. and W. H. Smith" across the square to W.H. Smith's former place of business on the southwest corner. His old building would be torn down and replaced by a "business house of hollow brick tile," which would then become the permanent home of Mr. Wagner's store and "another attractive addition to the east side of the square."

L. Debo moved his café business into "the building just about completed by Walter E. Wallace on the east side of the public square.

The latest in a series of fatal accidents on the new Hwy 66 between Burnet and Marble Falls claimed the life of E.G. Michel Jr., a prominent citizen of Marble Falls. The *Bulletin* estimated that this was the eighth fatality since the road had been completed "three or four years ago," and stated that seven of the victims had been from Marble Falls.

A January 24 article reported that a "blue norther" had struck Burnet County the previous Sunday, but that such storms were much less frequent than they had been "30, 40 or 50 years ago," when winters were "much colder."

On Valentine's Day, the *Bulletin* reported that "an abundance of rain has fallen" during the past week ("the best rains this section has had in a long time"), but that much more rain would be needed to "cope with a dry spring or summer."

The next week's headline was, "A Splendid Season," as three more inches of rain had fallen around the county. That same week, the *Bulletin* reported that four area leaders had been appointed as directors for the new Lower Colorado River Authority: Roy Fry and Tom Ferguson from Burnet, Roy Inks from Llano and J. Key from Lampasas.

On February 28, the *Bulletin* listed several new construction projects in Burnet: Waddell Northington was building "a very handsome cottage" on his property "northeast of the Christian Church."

Miss Pearl Whitley was looking for a good carpenter to build a house on property in the northeast section of Burnet, which she had recently purchased from Bill Chamberlain. Tommie White had torn down the "residence property" on his recently acquired land on the north side of the square, and was planning a "stucco business house." He also had plans to remodel the rock building next door. Tommie Ferguson was about to remodel a home he had purchased "on the block south of the school buildings," and Ollie Biggs had just completed a "very attractive fence" on his Hwy 66 property in southwest Burnet.

That week's paper also announced that Roy Fry had been elected "permanent chairman" of the LCRA (he had been serving as "temporary chairman") and Lee Clark (also of Burnet) had been named Treasurer.

Members of the Burnet County Commissioners Court and local business leaders (apparently including the publisher of the *Bulletin*) attended a dinner in the officers' headquarters dining room at Longhorn Cavern State Park. First on the program was a tour of the cave, and the *Bulletin* article described an amazing amount of progress by the CCC Boys, even though their equipment was quite primitive. Many tons of dirt and bat guano were hoisted in huge buckets on cables, some human powered, some powered by a gasoline engine. The new limestone-and-cypress administration building was taking shape, and three miles of Park Road 4 was "in good shape," with quite a few cement culverts already completed, even though most of the work was done with "picks, shovels and wheelbarrows."

On March 4, Mayor W.C. Galloway announced his candidacy for re-election; his main issue was the long-hoped-for water works, which he believed he could make a reality in his next term.

On March 21, a big business deal made front-page news. A new company, formed by J.F. Barnes of Waco, T.O. Whitaker of Burnet and others, purchased the Wm. P. Carey Lumber Co., one of Burnet's oldest businesses, and merged it with Mr. Whitaker's Home Lumber Co.

Also that week, the *Bulletin* reported a severe dust storm on the previous Saturday. The story said, "it completely obliterated the sun for several hours, and destroyed the visibility except for a short distance." It quoted other newspapers which had reported that the dust was coming from the Texas panhandle and surrounding states.

And a visit from Bill Daugherty confirmed a previous article in which the *Bulletin* had guessed that the two immense granite slabs for the federal building in Dallas had come from the Shannon Quarry, a few miles west of Burnet. Mr. Daugherty recalled in detail the challenges of hauling those slabs to the railroad in Burnet.

An April 4 article reported that work was progressing rapidly on the last section of Hwy 66 in northern Burnet County. The *Bulletin* predicted that it would become one of the most heavily travelled highways in Texas.

A week later, the Texas Highway Department approved the construction of a bridge across the Colorado River (just below Buchanan Dam) and a scenic lakeshore highway "skirting Lake Buchanan for a distance of approximately 10 miles" in Llano County. The order also approved the relocation of Hwy 29 in western Burnet County, and the article noted that "several miles of the old unpaved winding road will be submerged by the lake." A condition of the order was that the commissioners court would not "come back and seek additional state money for building a 2.5-mile shorter cut-off road away from the lake."

A very interesting article on April 18 reported that the average price of a car had decreased from $1,662 in 1909 to $678 in 1934, and added that the 1934 car was better looking, more durable and cheaper to operate. At the same time, the average price of a house had increased from $2,173 to $4,020! The article argued that even though "the 1934 house is a better structure from the standpoint of heating, insulation, plumbing, etc., the difference in cost cannot be attributed to that."

On April 25, the paper reported that the section of Hwy 66 completed the previous year (the first 7 or 8 miles north from Burnet city limits) would be topped with asphalt "at an early date." The article explained that the section between Burnet and Marble Falls was too narrow for topping, and would have to wait until it had been widened. The article under that one reported that Ardie Loveless was building a filling station on Hwy 66 in Burnet, "across the street west from the old Guthrie-Howell property."

That night (as reported in the next week's paper) burglars broke into Dave Kleen's hardware store. Night watchman Jake Clements was near the Biggs Meat Market on the north side of the square, and saw someone entering the front door. Even though he thought it was probably the owner, he had "started across to investigate" when he saw three men run out and escape in a car that was parked between the *Bulletin* office and the Guthrie-Howell building. They had taken four guns and several boxes of ammunition (a $128 total value) in less than a minute, leading everyone to assume that they knew exactly what they wanted and where it would be. There were no other obvious clues, and no one had seen which way the car had gone on Hwy 66.

Other stories that week reported that "good rains" had fallen in parts of the county, and that (as people came to Burnet looking for work) more residences were needed. Also, a re-printed article from the *Menard Messenger* told how a local rancher had sold 500 head of four- and five-year-old steers for the pre-depression price of seven and a half cents per pound to a buyer from Oklahoma.

But the very next week came news that three men had been arrested in East St. Louis for stealing a car, and they had been in possession of the guns from Kleen Hardware! The three were escapees from the Dallas jail.

That same week's paper reported more "Great Rains in Burnet County," and spirits were high among local farmers and ranchers. Also that week, there was an ad for Longhorn Tailor Shop (M.E. Phillips, Mgr.), announcing that the business had moved "to the north side of the public square."

The May 16 paper predicted a "bitter fight" ahead as a constitutional amendment to repeal prohibition would be up for a vote on August 24.

On May 23, an article reported that the LCRA board would meet in Austin to plan "an early start of work to complete Buchanan Dam and build other power dams in the Colorado River under the recently granted $20 million federal works allotment." Fegles Construction, which had left all its equipment at the dam site in 1932, was one of the bidders for the new contract, and the *Bulletin* wished them well (hoping that Fegles would be able to start work more quickly than anyone else).

Another article that week was headlined, "Colorado River on a Rampage." Some Marble Falls residents believed it was at a record level. The following week reported some sad news from Kingsland; a young man named Mark Green, who had come to Kingsland a few weeks earlier to work for a "Houston gravel concern," drowned in the river. The article said that he was an excellent swimmer, but he "dived in head first, and failed to come to the top of the water." His body was discovered about an hour later.

There was some good news on May 30; an article reported that wool prices had rebounded from a low of around 17 cents per pound to about 25 cents that week. Mohair prices were also on the rise, and hogs were selling for more than they had since 1930. The article continued, "With two or three fair rains in June, this country will become more prosperous than it has since 1929 and the relief program should be entirely eliminated or greatly curtailed."

Just a week later, the headline said, "Too Much Rain!" The story began with, "Who would have thought a month ago that many of the farmers in this county would be ready to acknowledge that we are having too much rain?"

Another item that week reported that the name of "Highway No. 66" had been changed to "The American Legion Memorial Highway of Texas."

On June 13, a front-page story noted that the Burnet County Relief office was cultivating a 55-acre garden at Marble Falls, where "thousands of pounds of vegetables" were raised and canned. Also, some of the people who were benefiting from "relief" were making winter clothes for others who were in need.

A column by publisher L.C. Chamberlain featured memories of years gone by. He told how he had been personally acquainted with Burnet pioneers like S.E. Holland (Burnet's first settler, who was elected County Treasurer in 1852) and John Jennings, who served on the county's first Commissioners Court. He recalled his first-ever telephone conversation: "I was skittish about it as a locoed mule, and when the answer came back to me I jumped ten feet high and called for help." He also remembered being "inside the first log cabin, on Cow Creek, built in Burnet County."

The biggest news items on June 20 were the death of Burnet pioneer (and longtime leading citizen) Captain T.E. Hammond, and the postponement of Burnet's big Trade Day event. Almost as an afterthought, a story lower on the front page was headlined, "Angry

Waters Destroy Marble Falls Bridge." That story began: "Last Friday afternoon about 4 p.m. the bridge on Highway 66 across the Colorado River at Marble Falls was washed away by flood waters coming from the Llano River and its tributaries. About noon, the same day, the bridge across the Llano River, in Llano, also went down." The 670-foot Marble Falls bridge had been built in 1891.

Another story reported that a small railroad bridge across a stream between Kingsland and Llano was washed out with about a mile of track, and a freight train was marooned in that section for three or four days. Kingsland's Campa Pajama resort was "washed away," and other buildings in town were damaged.

An assessment of flood damages in Burnet County was presented to the Commissioners Court the following week. The largest item, by far, was "Pecan damage to crops and trees," for $3 million. Bridges and roads came next, at just $100,000. The total damages were assessed at $3,733,000.

The month of June ended with a "mass meeting" on the Burnet square to discuss the future route of Highway 29. Engineers from the highway department had already decided on a route between the square and the schools, and despite many objections (including those of Publisher L.C. Chamberlain), their opinions carried the day.

Ross Johnson was appointed Postmaster at Burnet, and he selected Vernon Greer as his assistant. Mr. Johnson was the grandson of Adam Rankin Johnson, and had been a World War veteran, a professional baseball player and a newspaper editor before returning to Burnet in 1932. He replaced Mrs. V.P. Gibbs, who had served as Postmaster for the previous 12 years.

The *Marble Falls Messenger* reported that construction was underway on a 12 x 38 foot ferry (to be pulled by a tugboat brought from the coast) which would be operated "on the lake above the dam" to keep traffic flowing on Hwy 66 until a new bridge could be completed. In the meantime, local businessmen had offered free boat service for people and freight at 30-minute intervals all day.

And *The Llano News* reported that a temporary "low-water" bridge had been opened beside the ruins of the old bridge across the Llano River, and it could actually handle much heavier loads (granite, etc.) than the old bridge.

Mayor W.C. Galloway received an encouraging letter (dated

July 11) from Congressman Buchanan, assuring him that an additional loan of $6,000 would soon be approved for the Burnet water works (apparently no bids had come in low enough to fit the previous grant and loan).

The *Austin Statesman* reported (in an article re-printed by the *Bulletin* on July 25) that plans had been ordered for a new Hwy 29 bridge "across the Colorado River below Buchanan Dam, to replace Bluffton bridge which will be inundated by Lake Buchanan, and for construction of the relocated highway from near Burnet to the dam. The county will furnish fenced right of way." The highway commission also allotted $2,000 for asphalt surfacing of Hwy 66 inside Burnet city limits.

An August 1 article reported that federal public works administrator Harold Ickes had signed a contract with the LCRA confirming the $20,000,000 loan which would pay for several dams along the Colorado River. The *Austin American* speculated that work on the dam could resume as quickly as two weeks. Fargo Engineering, which had prepared the original plans for the dam, had already been re-hired as consulting engineers, and negotiations were underway with Fegles Construction, whose equipment was already in place at the site.

On August 8, the sad news was reported that Roy Inks, of Llano, had died in a San Antonio hospital the previous Sunday. Mr. Inks was an influential businessman who had served as mayor of Llano and was a board member at the LCRA.

The big news on August 15 was that the paving of Burnet's public square had begun. The *Bulletin* gave much of the credit for this enormous improvement to Waddell Northington, who "took the bull by the horns and made the contemplated project an actuality." The cost of paving would be shared by the city, the county, "those owning property facing the square," and contributions from other citizens. The *Bulletin*, whose office faced Main Street on the southwest corner of the square, explained that its contribution would go toward paving on Main Street and the "the street running north of the building to Highway 66."

Also that week, publisher L.C. Chamberlain reported that he had made his first trip along the just-finished Hwy 66 from Burnet to Lampasas. He pronounced it "a splendid road in every respect," and said that (even though it had taken twenty years since it was first proposed) "it is appreciated just the same."

On August 22, an article sadly informed the citizens of Burnet that Mrs. Sarah Martin, the daughter of Burnet pioneer Logan Vandeveer and Burnet County's oldest resident, had passed away on August 19. She had lived in Burnet for 89 years, and had been able to recount most of the county's history by first-hand memory.

Mark Hearn reported to the *Bulletin* that the highway department had surveyed plots for five roadside parks along Highway 66 in Burnet County (plus one small park already built at Honey Creek), and that work should begin soon. The parks averaged about two acres each.

The Red & White grocery store, owned by F.L. Parks, advertised a list of specials; it included "golden ripe" bananas at a dime a dozen, two pounds of seedless grapes for 15 cents, two "large packages" of corn flakes for 17 cents and two dozen medium-sized oranges for 29 cents.

The LCRA reported that Clarence McDonough, chief engineer of the federal public works administration, would serve as general manager for the Buchanan Dam project. He was widely known and respected; his services were donated by Public Works Administrator Harold Ickes.

The *Bulletin* called for volunteers to help in "improving the road from this place to Buchanan Dam," citing its poor condition and its "imperative necessity" to the town. A work party was to be organized within the next few days.

An August 29 article reported that a "new rural telephone line" was now in use between Burnet and Lampasas. The line ran "along Highway 66 all the way, and is placed on good cedar posts amply high." It was a joint project of the telephone companies in both towns.

Also that week, the Burnet Lumber Company completed some "extensive improvements," including two new rooms at their office and a "nice garage at their residence building." The company also "added 60 feet to their lumber sheds" and "added greatly to their stocks of lumber and building supplies."

The Burnet Furniture Company ordered a new ambulance from the National Hearse and Ambulance Co. It was expected to arrive in about three weeks. Their one ambulance had previously served

Burnet's entire "trade territory," and was unable to keep up with recent demand.

The Burnet Chamber of Commerce held its monthly meeting on Monday, September 9. Scott Edman reported that Commissioner R.U. Fraser had graded the road to Buchanan Dam, but that it probably would have to be redone any time there was a heavy rain. Citizens would be asked to chip in for cattle guards along the route. City Commissioner J.W. Scott suggested that "tailings from the rock crusher near town be obtained and used on the sidewalks from the square to the school buildings and depot" and volunteered his truck for hauling. F.H. Hammond suggested that "old, unsightly vacant barns" along Hwy 66 should be removed, and Mrs. Ernest Craddock reported that her housing committee was finding accommodations for people moving to Burnet.

Anxiety was building over delays in the resumption of work at Buchanan Dam, and the *Bulletin* reported that even Roy Fry, a local merchant who was also serving as LCRA chairman, did not know exactly when it would begin.

Another September 12 article speculated that "continued rains" would have a bad effect on the cotton crop, since worms and insects were thriving in the wet weather. And another article commented sadly on the recent assassination of Senator Huey Long in Louisiana.

A flood in Lampasas County killed "considerable livestock" and damaged merchandise stored in shop basements around the Lampasas square.

The Estates Development Company purchased a tract of land from L.L. Baker, covering both sides of Morgan Creek as it entered the soon-to-be Lake Buchanan. The plan was to subdivide the scenic property into quarter-acre lots and provide stables, tennis courts, etc. for those who wished to build homes in the new "Baker Estates."

Dal Chamberlain continued to improve his Burnet Tourist Camp, adding attractive new cottages to the park near the Hamilton Creek bridge on Hwy 66. The *Bulletin* observed that the new business had struggled for the first two or three years, but now was "enjoying a splendid patronage."

A large ad and a news story announced the opening of the new Oaks Addition, on both sides of Hwy 66 just north of Burnet city limits. The new subdivision, financed by Fielding Hammond, Charles

Schnabel and Mark Hearn, would offer water and electric lines to each of the "spacious lots." Construction was just beginning on the first home, a "beautiful rock-veneer building with a tile roof."

Roy Fry began the installation of a new marble front with plate glass windows at his drug store on the square. And a small news item reminded readers that there was a free night school in Burnet where experienced tradesmen would "take an interest in the advancement of any one who may wish to take up the work."

Burnet's new hospital, "situated in the Edman property just north of the school buildings," scheduled a grand opening on October 3. It was owned by Dr. Hansford Brownlee of Austin, a Burnet native and the brother of State Representative Houghton Brownlee.

Despite some earlier concerns about the effect of all the rain on Burnet County's crop, most area farmers were reporting "fair to good" crops (except in the eastern parts of the county).

Paving was underway on stretches of Hwy 66 – inside Burnet city limits and for about eight miles north – and the *Bulletin* called it "about as pretty a piece of work as could be found anywhere."

Burnet High School's football team defeated Killeen 20 to 0, and looked forward to its next game, a home game against Round Rock (at 3:30 p.m. on Friday at School Park). Admission to the game was 15 cents for students and a quarter for adults.

H.R. Shelby, of N & S Grocery, offered (in a front-page ad) to "Fill your Picnic Basket for the Old Settlers Re-Union," scheduled for that weekend at Houghton Brownlee's ranch.

There was paving going on October 10, and the *Bulletin* predicted that South Main Street would be paved by the end of the week "provided the weather is suitable." And about 30 men were put to work refurbishing housing and cleaning up around the site of Buchanan Dam.

A re-printed article from *The Llano News* reported that a "reconnaissance of the proposed lakeshore drive" had been completed. The road would be about ten miles long, and at one point would offer a good view of the dam.

The Chamber of Commerce voted to use $100 left over from paving funds to build a road to Buchanan Dam through Hoover Valley, and formed a committee to work with Congressman Buchanan to "secure acreage" for a national park in northwestern Burnet County.

An October 17 list of blocks paved during the recent program included: the square, eleven and a half blocks of Main Street, three blocks of Depot Street, one block from the square to the Baptist Church and three one-block connections between Main Street and Hwy 66.

A vote on issuing bonds to pay for a municipal water works passed by an overwhelming 154 to 5 margin.

A wage scale was published on October 24 for workers at Buchanan Dam. Pay ranged from 40 cents per hour for an "Engineer's Helper" to $1.50 per hour for a "Revolving Derrick Operator." The average wage seemed to be about 80 cents.

The Texas Centennial Board appropriated $1,000 to "restore old Fort Crogan." The article writer could "remember when most of the fort buildings were intact," but lamented that "people did not realize the historical value," and "at the present time not a trace of some of them are left."

M.B. Edwards, of Georgetown, opened a meat market in the Wallace building on the east side of the Burnet square. He hired Tom Nesbitt to manage the market.

Hage & Co. opened a new dry goods store at the "Guthrie-Howell Corner" in Burnet, advertising a wide variety of merchandise priced from five cents to five dollars. A gallon of house paint was $1.59, ladies' leather dress shoes were $1.96 and 8-quart galvanized buckets were just 15 cents each.

Night watchman Jake Clements was able (with the help of volunteer firefighters Frank and Ren Nichols) to catch a fire at the Silver Grill Café before it caused major damage. It was just past midnight on Tuesday, October 29, when Mr. Clements smelled something burning and discovered "a heater under a coffee urn becoming unruly in some way." He alerted the Nichols brothers, who were "engaged in some remodeling work on Tom Ferguson's office on the north side of the square." They ran for the fire station and had a truck at the café within a minute or two. The fire was still small enough to be put out with fire extinguishers. The article mentioned that Mr. Clements was worth many times the meager salary he received, which was "made up entirely by private subscription."

W.H. Smith celebrated the 1st anniversary of his dry goods store with a big sale on November 2. Among the specials were "Men's

Sanfordized Overalls" for $1.25 per pair, children's tennis shoes for "39 cents up" and 66 x 80 "Part Wool Blankets – Worth Much More" for $1.98.

The Humble Filling Station, formerly operated by R.S. Bean, was purchased by M.E. Delong, who hired Lee Odiorne Jr. to manage it. They asked the public "for a continuance of the splendid business that the station has enjoyed" and hoped "to make many new customers."

A public works project was approved in Washington D.C. to begin clearing timber from the planned Lake Buchanan basin. The project would be under the direction of the Texas Works Progress administrator, W.P. Drought. The *Bulletin* lamented the fact that much of the "multiplied thousands of cords of wood" would have to be burned in place because the cost of hauling was more than the wood was worth.

The new Jones-Manor funeral home, which featured all the latest advances, including a large and comfortable chapel, held an Open House on November 2 and 3. More than 600 visitors toured the facility; they were greeted by the owners and employees Gene and Benita Clements. Each "gentleman visitor" was given a cigar, and each of the ladies a carnation.

"Quite a number" of men were working at Buchanan Dam by the beginning of November, "getting things in shape for construction activities," but no one seemed to know exactly when that construction would start.

The Burnet Automobile Company, on Highway No. 66, advertised "late model Dodges, Plymouths, Chevrolets, Fords, and many other cars" for "$50 -- $75 -- $100." J.R. Reed and A. Lee Lackey were the men to call.

An article titled, "1935 Crops," reported that the total cotton yield for the county was down, but for some farmers in the center of the county, "a number of farmers made the best cotton they had produced in years." Cotton prices had risen to 11 or 12 cents per pound, and corn crops were good around the county. The *Bulletin* opined that "the county as a whole is in better shape to face the future than for many years."

A November 21 article reported that the Public Works Administration had allotted a loan of $74,000 and a grant of $61,000 to build a new courthouse and jail in Burnet.

Another article that week described progress at Longhorn Cavern State Park. The new administration building was the most obvious improvement; it was built of "stone, logs and cypress slabs," and (in the writer's opinion) "should be good for a century or longer." In addition to attractive design, it featured "well furnished ladies and gentlemen's rest rooms, an observatory on the top floor and a nice office" for cavern manager Hob Galloway. The CCC Camp was "as neat and clean as a parlor," and featured a westward view "as beautiful and picturesque as can be found anywhere."

Mayor W.C. Galloway "signed numerous documents" clearing the way for construction of the municipal water works. The *Bulletin* spoke favorably of the project, pointing out that it would employ quite a few locals and expressing the opinion that it would be "the greatest public improvement the town has ever made."

The E.E. Greathouse cotton gin set a new record with 914 bales ginned, and the *Bulletin* expected that the total would top 1,000 by year's end. The article explained that the Greathouse gin was the best and most efficient cotton gin around, and that it attracted farmers from a greater distance than any previous gin in Burnet.

A November 28 article reported that volunteer firefighter Frank Nichols had been severely injured in a fall from the fire truck as it raced up Hwy 66 to a fire at the residence of Will Moore. Nichols was trying to "unfasten a valve" to prepare for use as soon as they arrived, but a hook he was holding on to gave way, and he fell on the pavement. The article said he had been taken to the new Burnet Hospital for "x-ray pictures," and that "it is likely that he will be laid up for some time." A collection was being taken to help pay his expenses.

A re-printed article from the *Austin Statesman* announced on November 28 that federal administrator Harold Ickes had approved a plan for the Buchanan Dam's completion. The article indicated that this was one more step in the right direction, and work should begin "within a few days" on the half-finished dam.

An ad that week announced that Granite Station, on Hwy 66, was now the Burnet dealer for Mohawk Tires, the "Best Name in Tires for 22 Years."

On December 5, a front-page article in the *Bulletin* reported that the Burnet Automobile Company had torn down the old warehouse building on Hwy 66, which they had purchased from the estate of Mrs. T.W. Gibbs, and was building a "handsome, up-to-date garage and show room on the property."

Another front-page article described a letter sent from Governor Jose Castells of Chaco, Argentina, to Ross Johnson Jr. Young Ross was a cousin of Buddy Root, whose parents lived in the governor's province. When Governor Castells was visiting in Austin, he had requested a meeting, and two weeks later, Ross received a letter from him. Excerpts from the letter said, "It was really a great pleasure for me to meet you at Austin," and "I will tell your cousin Buddy of the very important conversation we had about planes, and I promise to send some pictures of my plane."

On December 12, a report was printed from the recent Chamber of Commerce meeting. A possible new courthouse was discussed, and LCRA Chairman Roy Fry reported that a contract would soon be let for a second dam to be built three or four miles south of Buchanan Dam on the "old Arnold site." The expected cost of the second dam was $1,000,000.

Tommie White offered office space in Burnet for "dam officials," and Waddell Northington volunteered to furnish it. The Chamber also voted to ask the city and county for funds to supplement the salary of night watchman Jake Clements, and made a contribution of $5 to help produce a pamphlet to "describe the merits of Federal Highway No. 281 from the Gulf of Mexico to Canada." The article pointed out that "this is the same as State Highway 66 in Texas."

The Burnet County Commissioners Court ordered an election for December 21 "to determine whether or not bonds of said county in the sum of $74,000 shall be issued for the purpose of the construction of a courthouse and repairs and improvements to the jail. Only qualified property taxpayers are eligible to vote in this election." It was estimated that the bonds would result in an increase of five cents per $100 valuation in the city's property taxes.

An article the following week urged voters to approve the bonds, arguing that a new courthouse would be needed soon anyway, and that this was the only time they could expect the federal government to bear almost half the cost.

An ad for the Burnet Automobile Company bragged about the new 1936 Plymouth for its safety, comfort, hydraulic brakes and fuel economy (18-24 mpg). Prices ranged from $667 to $747.

Luke Hearn (who had been living in Marble Falls) purchased the Northside Meat Market from Ollie Biggs.

Roy Fry's prediction came true, and the LCRA called for bids on the "Arnold Dam," named for Austin engineer Ward Arnold, who had chosen the site several years earlier. It would be 1,700 feet wide and 67 feet high. Its cost was expected to be around $1.1 million. The LCRA also called for bids on clearing a strip around the edge of Lake Buchanan, extending from the "full" water line to 60 feet lower elevation. A public works program had been approved for the project, but "insufficient relief labor was available in Burnet and Llano Counties to do the job."

The Burn-Tex Theatre announced that it would give away a saddle, a Navajo blanket and bridle worth $100 on Christmas Day, causing excitement all around town.

Chairman Roy Fry, of the LCRA, declared a January 15 "deadline" for resumption of the construction at Buchanan Dam and for signing a contract to build the Arnold Dam.

The day after Christmas, the *Bulletin* reported that bonds to help build a new courthouse had passed by a margin of 81 votes countywide. In Burnet, the margin was much larger; 236 votes for, and 36 votes against. Bertram and Spicewood were solidly opposed to the new bonds, which also would cover upgrades at the county jail. That was 1935.

CHAPTER NINE

Burnet in 1936

The *Burnet Bulletin* took another look at Burnet County's prospects in 1936 and, if anything, it was more optimistic than it had been in 1931. An article in the January 9 edition compared conditions with its appraisal from five years earlier.

First of all, the two dams were budgeted to cost $20 million (mostly for labor), an investment four times as big as the $5 million originally estimated for the Hamilton Dam. Secondly, the dams would necessitate the clearing of thousands of acres in the lake basin, Highway 29 would have to be rerouted through the rugged hills of western Burnet County, and a much longer new bridge would be required to cross Inks Lake below Buchanan Dam. Thirdly, power lines would have to be built all over the county to provide access to the generated electricity. Fourth, the new Highway 66 from San Antonio had arrived in Burnet, and was being extended to Lampasas (the article noted "the absence of a bridge over the Colorado River in Marble Falls" since the flood of 1935 had washed away the old bridge). Fifth, the revived economy would allow the refurbishing and reopening of the Frank C. Pavitte Lead Mine in northwestern Burnet County, a process which would require another new road and more new power lines. Sixth, the city of Burnet was about to start work on a new "waterworks." And lastly, the county had obtained funding for a new courthouse to replace the aging limestone building on the square in Burnet.

The 1874 courthouse, pictured here in its earlier years, was in very poor condition by 1935. Burnet residents voted overwhelmingly to approve bonds for a "modern" courthouse, and the old building was torn down in 1936.

This time, the *Bulletin* was right on the money, and the weekly paper was filled with (almost all) good news for at least the next three years.

On January 16, 1936, a news article reported that the name of the Arnold Dam (which had never been "officially" named) had been changed to honor Roy B. Inks, the former mayor of Llano. Mayor Inks had worked diligently to make the dams a reality, then had died suddenly in 1935, without ever seeing the results of his effort.

Another article in that same paper noted that M.G. Schnabel, of Burnet, would celebrate his 90th birthday that day. Mr. Schnabel had been born in Germany, but came to Texas at age 21, and had been in the "bakery and grocery business in this place" since 1883, "in business in Burnet many years longer than any other person."

At the end of January, an article headlined, "New Buildings and Improvements," mentioned the new Burnet Hospital on N. Water St., a new neon sign that "Mr. White" had installed on the Burn-Tex Theatre and reported that "the Burnet Automobile Company is progressing rapidly on their new building, situated west of the public square on Highway 66." Another article raved about "W.A. Kroeger's handsome new residence in the northwestern part of town," which was almost completed at the time. "It is almost a mansion in size," the writer continued, "and is complete and attractive in every detail. Mr. and Mrs. Kroeger have one daughter and several sons. Their home is ample in size and arrangements to take care of all of them."

It was the end of an era when the *Bulletin's* main front-page article on February 15 was titled, "Goodbye Old Courthouse Building." It pointed out that "the wrecking of the old courthouse will remove one of the landmarks of Burnet County, and will cause a tinge of regret from many, although those familiar with the situation know that such was approaching an absolute necessity, if it had not already reached that point." County officials were spread around the square as demolition began. County Judge O.B. Zimmerman moved into "the rock building at the rear of Hage & Co's store," County Clerk Frank Atkinson and County Treasurer Lucy Lamon moved into the Masonic Hall, tax assessor/collector Cecil Humphries moved into the back of the brick First State Bank building; District Clerk Walter Wallace would have his office in the jail, and court would be held in the second-floor room of "Neuman's rock store building." The demolition was expected to take 40 days, and the construction of the new courthouse was predicted to take "several months."

Burnet was justly proud of its two impressive schools, which stood back-to-back on the block between Pierce and Boundary Streets, at Johnson Street, and the *Bulletin* included photos in a February edition. The fairly new brick high school faced west, and the imposing 1898 elementary school seemed to face diagonally to the southeast behind the high school.

There was much discussion as to the new location of Hwy 29. Many seemed to want the highway to go through the Burnet Square and follow the Hoover Valley Road to a new bridge "as close as possible to the Roy Inks Dam." That would make the trip to Llano a mile longer, but "would serve more citizens of Burnet County."

The two new dams were the biggest news in Burnet in the spring of 1936. A front-page story in the *Burnet Bulletin* that March described the expectations for Lake Buchanan: the tentative date for the completion of the dam was January 1, 1938, and the projected time for filling the lake was one year after that. An expert opined that because of "the type of soil being covered," and because "waves three or four feet high will cut down all the irregularities near the shore," there would be sandy beaches along the shore on the Llano County side of the lake. Workers were expected to begin clearing the "reservoir for the Buchanan Dam lake" sometime in April. In the same paper, an article described an attractive "new annex to Schnabel's Bakery," which was under construction on Main Street in Burnet.

At the end of March, an article mentioned that Parks Chairman Mark Hearn was involved in an ongoing effort to have the buildings of old Fort Croghan restored as part of the Texas Centennial celebration. He had received a letter from "Henry Hutchings, Secty.," saying, "The restoration of old Fort Croghan was certified to the United States Texas Centennial Commission and will, I believe, be accepted by them." The article continued, "Mr. Hearn also assures the *Bulletin* that the parks along Hwy 66 will be built and improved at no distant date. There will be four new parks established in Burnet County – one not far from the Lampasas County line, the second just south of the town of Burnet, the third beyond the railroad crossing on Houghton Brownlee's ranch, and the fourth on the south bank of the Colorado River at Marble Falls."

On April 2, 1936, the *Bulletin* reported that the county had received an advance payment from the U.S. Treasury for construction of a new courthouse, and that work was expected to begin "within the next few days." Completion of the project was expected by December 1. Work had already started on a new water system; both projects were expected to employ quite a few workers in Burnet (in addition to the hundreds employed at the dams). The article went on to note that a reporter had counted ninety structures (homes and businesses) which had been completed within the past two years or were currently under construction. Many of those homes were actually in the "Oaks Addition" north of town, but many were on the south and east sides of the town. The *Bulletin* estimated that the population of Burnet had increased by about 500 in the past two or three years, and added: "There is still a demand for living quarters; every business house is occupied, there is not a vacant residence in town, and many people have cut their homes into apartments to help relieve the clamor for places to live."

On April 16, the Burnet Chamber of Commerce announced that it was inviting committees from Bertram and Marble Falls to discuss the possibility of forming municipal light and power plants for the three towns. Thomas G. Ferguson, who was a member of the LCRA board and president of the Burnet Chamber, estimated that Burnet was paying $1,300 per month to Texas Power & Light at the time; a new municipal power plant would cost $50,000, and could be "easily paid for in ten years."

On May 2, the State Highway Commission ordered that "the construction of grading and drainage structures on Highway 29 from the Williamson County line to Burnet, and from Burnet to the Llano County line be placed upon the 1937 Regular Federal Aid Program." The order was passed "on condition that the county will agree to obtain not less than 100-foot right-of-way on location approved by the State Highway Engineer." A "highway census" taken around the same time disclosed that an average of 687 cars and trucks passed "a certain point on Highway 66" (now 281) each day; 12 of the cars and 7 of the trucks were from outside the state. An average of five horse-drawn vehicles passed by the same point each day.

An interesting article in the May 9 *Bulletin* told of a visit by a man who had "attended school at this place when Prof. Russell was in charge," but had moved away twenty or thirty years earlier. He told a reporter that the town had changed so much "that if he had been cast into the town at night, he could not have told where he was if his life depended on it." The old courthouse was gone, and "the public square, which had been almost vacant on the east side, and partially so on the north and west," was "now completely built up, and there have been noticeable improvements on the south side."

Another article that month was headlined, "Court House work progressing," and "an office and tool checking room" had been built, as well as a "building to house the cement," and "a number of foundation holes have been dug." One column over, another article reported that 600 additional workers had been hired to work on the Buchanan Dam project, bringing the total to 900 currently employed there.

On July 9, the paper reported that "the greatest activity is being manifested in the Colorado River dam projects," and that "the LCRA has completed the task of taking over the Buchanan and Roy Inks projects from the U.S. Reclamation Bureau." It went on to say that "many new men have gone to work on the Buchanan Dam project this week, and the contractors for the Roy Inks Dam are on the ground ready to start when work orders are received."

This architect's drawing showed the future Burnet County courthouse to be built in 1936.

In the same issue, the *Bulletin* reported that "extensive progress" was being made on the "modernistic" new courthouse. The foundation had been completed, and "skeleton walls are being made in preparation for the granite. There has been erected a tower near the structure which will aid the employees in their work on the second story. Forms are being built for the pouring of cement in the walls, after which granite will be laid."

September 1 was set as the date that "the first storing of the water in the lake (Buchanan) will be started," and that "after that date, some twenty feet of water can be stored and more capacity will be afforded as fast as construction can be completed." An ad placed by the Burnet Chamber was addressed to employees working on the dams. It said, "In order to accommodate those working at Buchanan and Roy Inks dams, and their families, the merchants of Burnet will remain open every Friday and Saturday night until the wants of everyone are attended to. This plan is adopted because it is realized that many of those working on the dam projects are unable to get to town early in the evening."

Buchanan Dam was about half done when work stopped in 1932. It was 1936 before work resumed on the huge project.

Houghton Brownlee's campaign for the state senate issued a remarkable statement in the summer of 1936. One of his major issues was road construction for Central Texas, and his ad in the *Burnet Bulletin* said: "The counties of Llano, San Saba and Lampasas do not have a single foot of hard-surfaced roads. Burnet County has only about ten miles of hard-surfaced roads. . . These counties have not gotten a fair deal, and Mr. Brownlee promises not to forget them when elected from this district."

Even with the booming economy and multiple construction projects in Burnet, there was plenty of room for improvement; one of the priorities (shared by publisher Louis Coleman "L.C." Chamberlain, who had been running the *Burnet Bulletin* since 1898) was better roads. In an article in July of 1936, headlined, "Good Roads We Must Have," Chamberlain argued: "Things are not like they used to be. In the olden days, people did their trading at the town nearest to them, provided other things were equal. It is different now, and a few miles further does not make any difference to the average householder when he starts out to purchase his supplies. His major thought is the kind of road he must travel to reach his destination."

Events were already in motion to bring better roads to Burnet

County. Another article that same week told of progress on the new Marble Falls bridge; a ferry was the only way to cross the Colorado River on Hwy 66. The *Bulletin* reported that "work is going right along, and will be completed within a few weeks. It will be an immense structure, and the entire county should be proud of it."

A separate article told of a contract awarded to the Morgan Construction Company of Brady to pave 11.84 miles of Hwy 66 between Burnet and Lampasas for $42,000, and other articles reported "Work Started on the Roy Inks Dam" and "1,000 Men at work on Buchanan Dam Project." In the story, the *Bulletin* opined that "These people must all have clothing and groceries, and Burnet is getting its share of the business. The most potent factors for drawing trade to any given place are the roads that the customers must travel."

A fascinating front-page article on August 27 reported "Recent Improvement in Burnet." Some of the type is barely legible, so spelling of some names may be incorrect, but the gist is clear. It starts out, "Several new residences have been started in Burnet within the past few days," and continues as follows:

"On his property on Highway 66, in the southern part of town, L. Debo is building a new residence. This will be the third house on this property. The contractor is Ed Purcell. Dal Chamberlain has about completed five new attractive cabins for his Burnet Tourist Camp, just across Hamilton Creek on Highway 66. Mr. Walker has about completed a small residence in Roy Fry's field, just south of city limits.

Work was started Monday morning on a handsome duplex brick veneer residence for Miss Kate Sarrels, on her property in the southern part of town from which her home burned several weeks ago. Burnet has several rock houses, but this will be the first brick home in town, and promises to be a very handsome affair. M.W. Nolan is the contractor.

John Ferguson is erecting an attractive cottage in the southern part of town. The contractor is M.B. Cox. Mr. and Mrs. J.O. Cole have lately erected a duplex cottage near their residence in the eastern part of town, which is operated in connection with their boarding house. The Church of Christ house of worship is receiving a new covering of shingles.

An attractive cottage is being erected by Mrs. D. Skinner on the property near the school buildings, which she purchased several months ago from Mrs. H. Breazeale. O.C. Brady & Sons are the contractors. V. P. Gibbs is building a cottage on the southwest corner of the Landes property on North Main Street, which will be occupied by Mrs. Frank Landon and daughters, L.M. Fowler is the contractor. Mr. and Mrs. V.P. Gibbs have just completed a double two-story garage on their property near the school buildings. The upper story will be used for sleeping quarters.

A Texaco filling station has been started on the Sam McFarland property northwest of the public square, on Highway 66. L.M. Fowler is the contractor. Others who have built residences in Burnet since they received their bonus money in July are Denver Baker, in the southeastern part of town, Charley Keenan on Highway 66, and Jimmie Walker and Jack Barron in the southern part of town. These had been mentioned previously in the *Bulletin*, but it is not amiss to catalogue them with the late improvements.

In addition to the above improvements, there have been numerous other improvements of a minor nature lately, both on business and residence buildings. Burnet is destined to become quite a little city, and right now the people should begin to look for and encourage concerns to come here that will have permanent payrolls. Just what our population is at the present time is only guess work. Some of our citizens think it has doubled since the last census was taken in 1930. The *Bulletin* thinks such guesses are a little high."

The Colorado River and Highway 29 dominated the front pages of the *Burnet Bulletin* in the fall of 1936. A September 2 article, titled, "Pay Rolls at Buchanan and Roy Inks Dams," reported that more than 1,000 paychecks had been issued that week at Buchanan Dam and more than 200 at Inks Dam, totaling probably at least $50,000. A *Bulletin* reporter was "amazed at the tremendous work" done "within the past two months, since the Colorado River Authority took over the job." The main focus so far had been road construction and excavation; Brown & Root Construction was making good progress on its contract for "clearing the timber from Buchanan Dam basin." Concrete work on the dam was expected to be complete by August 1, 1937. The article ended by noting that "Burnet and other towns adjacent to the dam work are as lively as beehives."

A front-page editorial by publisher L.C. Chamberlain questioned a recent decision by the highway department to locate the new Hwy 29 a block north of the town square "between the public square and the school buildings." His main objections were that it would hurt local business and create a danger for school children. He made some very interesting points.

Hwy 29 approached Burnet from the southeast during the 1930s, entering the square on what would later become Jackson Street. Pictured here are newlyweds Vivian and Ren Nichols, who would be solid Burnet citizens for many years. They are posing with the highway marker in front of the David G. Burnet Hotel, just off the southeast corner of the square.

Photo courtesy of Karl Piehl

Refuting the argument that the streets around the square were too narrow for the new highway, he cited the highway through Liberty Hill's business district, where the streets were not even as wide as Burnet's. And to those who thought it would be too dangerous to have a highway running through the square, he said, "there has never been a fatal automobile accident on the public square of Burnet, nor on Highway 29 (the old Bertram Highway, which came under the narrow railroad underpass at the south end of Boundary Street, up to Jackson Street, then turned left toward the square) in its passage through the town." He added: "On the other hand, between Burnet and Marble Falls, where many people drive at break-neck speed, there have been numerous serious and several fatal accidents."

Mr. Chamberlain's other objection to the plan was that "probably three fourths of the school children of this district would have to cross (the new highway) three or four times daily. Many of these are little tots and become easily confused. If travel over this route would be as rapid and reckless, and it will be, as it is over 66 through town, school children will be in constant danger."

In another article the next week, Mr. Chamberlain argued that the people of Burnet should be allowed to decide the route of Hwy 29 through town. He added that "it is not narrow roads that are responsible for most car casualties, but fast roads. Occasionally a nitwit, whatever that is, drives through the public square at break-neck speed. During all hours of the day and night, people with fairly good judgement pass through town on Highway 66 as fast as their cars will go. It will be the same thing, and everybody knows it, if 29 is routed through Burnet between the public square and the school buildings." "On the other hand, if it goes through the public square, 900 of every 1,000 will slow down, if for no other reason than their own preservation."

A flood on the Colorado River took over the front pages at the end of September. About 16 inches of rain had fallen in San Angelo, and heavy rains (including 9 inches in Tow) fell all along the river. "At Bluffton," the *Bulletin* reported, "the water got within a foot or two of the floor of the bridge, which is 52 feet high. Mr. Chris Dorbandt, who has closely observed the rises of the river at Bluffton for at least 40 years, is of the opinion that the present rise surpassed any he has ever seen, unless it was in 1900, which was a very close second to the present rise. Dock Maxwell, who was raised on the river, thinks the present rise has a slight edge on the 1900 flood. Other notable rises in the Colorado within the past 50 years were in 1908 and 1922."

The bridge at Bluffton survived with slight damage to the approaches, but (unbeknownst to the residents of Burnet) the bridge at Tow was washed away in the flood. Tow was cut off from Burnet, with roads washed out and telephone lines knocked down, and it was two weeks before an article from Miss Verna Everett reported the loss in the *Bulletin*. She explained that the bridge had linked the two sides of Tow, and that the Burnet County side was "cut off from church, school, post office, jobs, and the men from their chewing tobacco."

In the meantime, roads were flooded in many locations in western Burnet County, and quite a few workers were trapped in Burnet, where they had gone shopping over the weekend. The Daugherty Branch in Burnet "got so high that the Burnet Fire Department became uneasy about the J.J. Boyce place, and about one o'clock assisted in removing Mrs. Boyce and other occupants of same." The article continued, "The water was several feet over the bridge on Highway 66, near the Boyce place. The people living in tents on Highway 29 at the Hamilton Creek crossing were removed by men from the highway department before their effects were washed away or any loss of life occurred. The Pentecostal tabernacle near the bridge across Hamilton in the southern part of town was washed away and the water got up to the church building."

Not everyone escaped safely. A 19-year-old "by the name of Williams" was drowned near the Inks Dam site, when he and two others (all workers at the dam construction site) tried to swim the river so they could go to the Burnet-Lampasas football game. The other two (a brother and a friend) were able to get back to the west bank of the river; the 19-year-old's body was found three days later, two miles past the Kingsland bridge.

That flood convinced the highway department that their plan to build the new Hwy 29 (along the old Hoover Valley Road route and across the Colorado River on a low-water crossing just below the Inks Dam) was not feasible. Although many Burnet County residents were opposed to the northern route, the decision was made around that time to adopt the route that we still travel in 2020.

A very interesting (but not too diplomatic) article in the October 6 *Bulletin* ("This and That," by Mrs. Jas. A. Jackson) described recent changes on the Burnet square. "The First State Bank still occupies its prominent corner with the pretentious new Burnet Hotel on the side at the same old hotel site. However, Willis Smith, our pioneer dry goods merchant, is just opposite his old stand and now occupies the former National Bank building. The Post Office, Guthrie Drug Store, Churchill's Hardware, Schnabel's and Roy Fry's Drugs all remain 'put.' There's a predominance of filling stations; three on the corners of North Main; a number of barber shops and beauty parlors, three garages, a jewelry store – not Wingren's, which is now a lunch room, of which there are several others; a number of groceries, novelty stores, dry goods and dress shops with a nice picture show on the east side."

"The Garrett Hotel, formerly the Jones House, enlarged and greatly improved, still serves the public. The new courthouse spreads conspicuously over the center block, the fine trees having been sacrificed in its construction. It is too early to determine its attractiveness though there is no doubt of its adequacy in the matter of room. Architecturally, it does not appeal to me – tho it will doubtless be very handsome when completed since, as I understand, it is to be faced with polished granite. Constructionally, it is of the streamlined style so much in vogue, and which holds little interest for me. I do not like streamlined anything – so glad streamlined girls are going out of fashion and plump curves are coming back."

The personal, conversational style of writing mirrored that of publisher L.C. Chamberlain, who often interspersed his news stories with personal observations (making the whole paper much more interesting to present-day readers). A personal tidbit was included in a November 5 story ("Not Like it Used to Be"), which noted that "youngsters in Burnet are not near so wild and destructive in Burnet as they used to be" on Halloween night, and that "Hansford Stapp's steps on his tin shop were dislocated to some extent and a few small houses" (outhouses, we are assuming!) were overturned, which with soap writing on a number of the plate glass windows and doors constituted the major portion of the mischief. The article continued with an unfortunately mostly illegible tale of the writer's escapades as a youth, which at least once got him in trouble with the law!

Much of Burnet's growth and prosperity in the middle of America's Great Depression was directly related to Franklin D. Roosevelt's "New Deal" programs, and Burnet County appreciated that fact. The November 7 issue of the *Burnet Bulletin* rejoiced in its reporting of FDR's landslide re-election. The polls were even more lopsided in Burnet County than in the rest of the country; unofficial numbers reported in the *Bulletin* were at least 517 for FDR, and just 23 for his opponent, Alfred Landon of Kansas.

A November 12 story reported that Mayor W.C. Galloway, after years of applications and negotiations, had received $31,173.08 from the Federal Reserve Bank in Dallas "to be used for the purpose of installing a water works system for the town of Burnet." In Mr. Chamberlain's opinion, the most important of "numerous benefits to the town" would be reduced fire insurance premiums. He spoke highly of the town's fire department (of which he was a charter member), and opined that "no town gets into the little city class without water works, and such is all that is lacking to make Burnet in a class with the most progressive towns in the state."

On November 19, one article told of a fundraising drive to repair roads from Burnet to the dam sites (Buchanan and Inks). It said, "The continued rains during the fall, coupled with the heavy traffic on the Hoover Valley road and on to the dam sites have placed these thoroughfares in a rough condition in many places, and their repair is an absolute necessity." It went on to praise the Chamber of Commerce and local businesses for helping the cause, and noted that Burnet now had a "splendid highway entering it from the north – 66." It continued, "It is not so good from the south, but it is due to be paved in that direction before many months." Hwy 29, from Bertram and Bluffton "is not so good in places, but is so far ahead of what we used to have that there is no great amount of grumbling from the natives."

The article noted that the state highway commission would receive bids on November 23 for the construction of a bridge across the Colorado River near Buchanan Dam, and that work on the project would probably begin early in the new year (1937). Also, there would be "an entirely new route for Highway 29" from Burnet to Llano, but (because the terrain was so rugged in western Burnet County) that highway would probably not be finished before the dams were completed.

Another November 19 article reported that "Burnet Will Probably Have Gas Within a Few Months." Mayor Galloway had informed the *Bulletin* that Burnet and several other area towns were negotiating with gas companies to run pipelines through Burnet, Llano and "adjacent counties." The writer of the article (presumably L.C. Chamberlain) recalled that people from the "black land" area of Texas, who used to speak dismissively of Burnet County as "the sticks," had changed their tune. "Not one of them now will deny the superiority of 'the sticks,'" he wrote. "We are now called by a more romantic name – Hill Billies – of which all of us are proud."

A smaller article in that same week's paper reported that "Burnet County's new courthouse is beginning to put on a magnificent and handsome appearance," although "bad and rainy weather" had put the project behind schedule.

Postmaster Ross Johnson reported that the post office would move "from its present site to the new Charley Schnabel building, adjoining Schnabel's Bakery and Grocery." At the same time, he added a new "Star Mail Route, down Mormon Mill Road and Hairston Creek Road, thence back to Burnet on Highway 29."

Burnet County far surpassed its $514.00 "quota" for the Democratic campaign fund in 1936. The *Bulletin* noted that "Perhaps no section of the country has received greater benefits from the Roosevelt administration than Burnet County, and that such is appreciated was shown by their contributions."

Warren C. Galloway served as Burnet's mayor through most of the 1930s.

The mayor and city commissioners entered into a contract (along with "Lampasas, Lometa, Goldthwaite, San Saba, Llano, Fredericksburg and several other towns") with a "Mr. Moore of Lubbock" to "install a gas system in the City of Burnet." Work was to begin within 90 days.

The Harvey Richey Motor Company remodeled the "Old McFarland Blacksmith Shop" and turned it into a Ford dealership. It offered the "Ford V-8 and the Lincoln Zephyr," and advertised "one of the best-equipped Ford Service Stations in this county."

Sometime in December, the new Marble Falls bridge was completed, and the *Bulletin* reported that it was "a very beautiful structure" with "a view of the falls and beautiful lake." The article also noted that traffic had been "greatly inconvenienced for more than 18 months" by the absence of a bridge on Highway 66, and that sometimes things "would become so congested at the ferry that it would take hours to get across the river."

After all the good news for Burnet in 1936, the year ended on a sad note. Mayor W.C. Galloway passed away (at the age of 80) on December 29, 1936; L.C. Chamberlain wrote a long and laudatory front-page article about the enormously popular and accomplished mayor, whose obituary said, "Dating almost from his arrival in Burnet, a period of about 54 years, Mr. Galloway was an important and leading factor in the business life of Burnet. He served Burnet County as Tax Collector and made an unusually efficient officer. Since the organization of the First State Bank of Burnet in 1908, and until his death, Mr. Galloway served as Cashier. For several years prior to his death, he had been mayor of Burnet, and took merited pride in the things that had been accomplished during his term of office, the greatest of which was the installation of the city water works system. It was during his tenure of office in which several miles of city paving was secured. During the dark days of the depression, Mr. Galloway took as much interest in city affairs as he did in his own business and the town's growth and development was a source of great pride to him."

The front-page article ended by saying, "Burnet will never seem the same to many people because of the passing of Warren Galloway." That was 1936, a momentous year in the history of Burnet.

CHAPTER TEN

Burnet in 1937

Construction at Buchanan and Inks Dams was winding down by the beginning of 1937, but Burnet continued to boom with the ongoing construction on Hwys 66 and 29. The bridge in Marble Falls had been completed at the end of 1936, but the Inks Lake bridge was just getting started. A new courthouse and new water works weren't quite finished in Burnet, and the CCC Boys were not yet finished with their work at Longhorn Cavern (including the section of Park Road 4 which would follow the east side of Inks Lake).

Burnet had a distinguished visitor in February, when Secretary of the Interior Harold L. Ickes came from Washington on the 19th to inspect the nearly completed dams. Just three days later, Burnet received the news that Congressman James F. Buchanan had died of a heart attack. He had been hugely instrumental in getting the dams approved, and the first and largest dam bore his name. The *Burnet Bulletin* lamented his passing, calling him the state's "most influential congressman" and praising the "bulldog tenacity" with which he pursued his goals.

Buchanan would be succeeded by an even more influential congressman when young and little-known Lyndon Baines Johnson quit his job as director of the National Youth Administration and campaigned feverishly as "President Roosevelt's man" to gain 28% of the vote and beat eight rivals for the vacated seat. Most of his votes came from the five Hill Country counties (including Burnet County), which were part of the 10th Congressional District at the time.

On April 5, 1937, a huge party was held at Longhorn Cavern to celebrate the 4th anniversary of the CCC project there. Burnet schools were closed for the occasion, and more than 3,000 people (from all around Texas) toured the cavern that day, with guides leading groups numbering up to 300 at a time, from 9 a.m. to 8 p.m.

A large ad in the *Bulletin* that month was titled, "Contractors Notice of Texas Highway Construction," and called for bids on "Grading, Drainage Structures and Select Material" to create 17.5 miles of new highway from "2.7 miles west of Burnet to .3 miles west of the Burnet/Williamson county line." The ad specified that bids would be based on pay rates of 75 cents per hour for "skilled labor," 45 cents for "intermediate grade" labor and 35 cents for "unskilled labor." Plans and specifications were available at the office of "E.B. Calvin, Resident Engineer" in Burnet, or from the State Highway Department in Austin.

Water Street was becoming a whole new business district since it had been chosen as the route for State Highway 66, and ads in the *Bulletin* that spring included the "Marathon Granite Station" (T.A. Loveless) and "The Shell Café" (specializing in chicken dinners – Mr. and Mrs. V.G. Heckmann) on Hwy 66. Another prominent ad was from LaForge Hardware (on the square), and mentioned "Fine Nesco Oil Stoves, Ovens, etc. Fishing Tackle will be here soon. We have some good Radio sets. We do Radio Repairing."

An April 1937 article reported that the number of cars registered in Burnet County had risen from 1,649 to 2,035 in the previous 12 months. Farm and commercial truck ownership had gone from 369 to 430, and the number of registered trailers had increased from 17 to 35. An editorial that same week discussed the new Hwy 29, and warned that the lives of Burnet's school children would be endangered several times every day "if people drive over it, when completed, at the rate some of them go through town on Hwy 66." The same article mentioned progress on Hwy 29 "west of Burnet," and "cement pouring on the new bridge to cross the Colorado River below Buchanan Dam." The writer opined that "it will require several months to complete this bridge, but it is likely that both the road and the bridge will be finished before the lake waters of Buchanan Dam overflows any of Hwy 29 between Burnet and Bluffton."

At the end of April, a news story reported that "Burnet's water works system was received Wednesday, April 21st, and is now in operation with Clen Shilling in charge." It went on to say that the system had "about 26,400 feet of different sizes of pipe. It started off with 107 customers, with 15 more waiting for meters." The system belonged to the U.S. government, and the cost would be paid through customers' water bills.

Another article mentioned that Stop signs had been authorized for streets entering the square and going from the square to Hwy 66 (Washington and Jackson Streets). The same resolution set a speed limit of 20 mph on "the public square or public streets of mid-city" and required all vehicles to be "operated or driven upon the right hand side of the street only."

A report from the "Burnet School Annual" listed record public school enrollment of 667 students (in all grades) for the 1936-37 school year. The previous record of 414 had been set in 1931-32, when construction first began on the "Hamilton Dam" (later renamed for Congressman Buchanan). It dipped to 333 for the 1932-33 school year, then rose to 351, 372 and 405 in the next three years. The spike in 1936-37 had led to severe overcrowding and class sizes "greater than that recommended by the State Department of Education." The annual commended teachers for going above and beyond the call of duty; it predicted that enrollment would dip again in 1937-38, but then grow steadily to set a new record five years into the future.

Later in May, the *Bulletin* reported that E.B. Calvin had "leased land that will border the Inks Dam Lake when it is filled," and had already started building a log cabin-styled camp house. Also, "Mr. Patterson, of the Patterson Jewelry Co.," had purchased the commissary building from the Inks Dam building site and was turning it into a camp house on his own leased Inks Lake property. The Bulletin described Mr. Patterson as "the most enthusiastic booster in this section of the great opportunities for Burnet that will follow the completion of Buchanan and Inks Dam. He thinks the business people of Burnet are too luke-warm over the prospects before them."

A June 10 headline declared, "Buchanan Lake Filling Up," and the accompanying article told how rains farther up the Colorado

River had led to a rapid rise in the lake level. It said, "Highway 29 at the Bluffton bridge was closed last Friday night on account of the water overflowing the approaches on the Burnet County side, and travel has been routed over the two bridges at Buchanan Dam. People traveling west quit Highway 29 two miles west of Burnet and travel the Hoover Valley-Kingsland county road until they reach the foot of the mountain when they take the Buchanan Dam Road. The Bluffton bridge is now under water and many think it doubtful if it will ever be uncovered. It has been reported that it would be used to repair the Kingsland bridge, but such a procedure may now be too late." The story continued by reporting that C. Dorbandt had moved his ranch houses to his "south pasture on Hwy 29," about three or four miles east of the river, and that many other property owners had likewise moved whatever they could, on both sides of the river.

This photo of the nearly completed Buchanan Dam was taken in June of 1937. The dedication of the two dams (Buchanan and Inks) was held that October.

Burnet was still a very busy place in the summer of 1937; although, Buchanan and Inks Dams were finished and area construction was focused more on roads and bridges than on dams and buildings. A July article in the *Burnet Bulletin* described "a vast lot of machinery, of the Morrison-Knudson Construction Company, the people that built the Roy Inks Dam, is now stored at the Burnet depot or is on cars ready for shipment when a decision is made as to its destination." The article included an interesting side story: Mr. Williams, who supervised the dam-building, had been staying with his wife and their 9-year-old son at the Burnet Hotel. He had to go east on a business trip, and they sent their son by train to stay with relatives in Washington State. Mrs.

Williams gave her son $8.00 for meals on the four-day trip, with the admonition that he was "not to let his meals consist entirely of hamburgers." He arrived safely in Washington, and wrote to his mystified mother that he had $5.06 left from his meal money!

An ad in the *Bulletin* that July solicited bids for the job of applying "Double Asphalt Surface Treatment" on 13.845 miles of Highway 66, "from southwest of Marble Falls to the south city limits of the town of Burnet." An accompanying article reported that "Highway 66 is already paved from Burnet to Lampasas, and this new work (when completed) will make a stretch of about 35 miles of consecutive paving. Close to 32 miles of this will be in Burnet County."

The *Bulletin* also mentioned Claude S. Shipp, "the big law out at Buchanan Dam." It said that he had "a large job keeping things straight out his way, but he does it in a manner that keeps friction at a minimum."

Another article said, "The editor of the *Burnet Bulletin* is finding it difficult to stay away from Buchanan Lake on Sundays, and occasionally comes out there after work time on weekdays. The main attraction to him is the motor boats on the lake; it is a great thrill to ride them as they skim rapidly through the water." It continued, "Last Sunday there were more than a half-dozen on the lake, and one of them ascended the river to two or three miles past Fall Creek."

That same article reported that thousands of people were already visiting the dam every week just to see the growing lake, and predicted that the area would become a popular tourist attraction once the lakes had been stocked with fish. It also reported that several new homes were being built along the future shoreline of Inks Lake, and that the new Hwy 29 was almost completed "to beyond the river," with a "magnificent bridge across the Colorado" just a few weeks from completion. The next week's paper (near the end of July) reported that traffic had been routed down the new highway, which "appears to be a nice piece of work, but it is an exceptionally crooked road. It will be some time before the bridge across the Colorado River is completed."

At the end of July, State Senator Houghton Brownlee gave a speech to the Llano Luncheon Club, urging citizens of Llano and Burnet Counties to take the initiative in creating "a great national park" on the shores of the two new lakes. He also voiced his opposition to the taxation of natural resources, which he feared would damage Llano County's economy, and told his audience that he would do his best to reverse a history of neglecting the highways in Llano County.

This photo of the "new" Burnet County Courthouse was taken soon after its completion in 1937.

Citizens of Burnet County were urged to attend a Highway Beautification meeting at the courthouse on August 10. The *Bulletin* pointed out that the federal government had already allocated funds, but if Burnet County did not come up with a good plan, the money would be spent elsewhere.

In August of 1937, County Attorney Bill S. Watkins reported that work would soon begin on an 8-mile stretch of highway along the shore of Lake Buchanan, linking the old highway from Llano to the new highway from Burnet. The $70,000 work order did not include paving the road, but officials felt certain that "topping will not be long delayed." Another August article predicted that the new lakes would be stocked with millions of fish "as soon as necessary funds are available," and that fishing would bring "thousands of tourists from all over the state and the nation."

Tragedy struck Burnet near the end of August. The original Methodist church at the intersection of Polk and Water Streets had lost much of its parking area when those two streets became the main highways through town, and a new church was under construction at Johnson and Main when workers began to tear down the old building. Virgil D. Allen and Bill Kroeger were inside the half-gone building when a wall fell on top of them, knocking them both down and pinning them to the floor. They were both unconscious when witnesses reached them.

As the Burnet Furniture Company ambulance rushed the two victims to the Lampasas Hospital, Bill Kroeger regained consciousness; he was well enough to help carry Mr. Allen into the hospital when they arrived. Mr. Allen never regained consciousness, and died early the next morning.

The summer of 1937 ended with the announcement of a new fish hatchery to be constructed on the Burnet County side of the Colorado River, just below Inks Dam. Congressman Lyndon Johnson had invited officials from the Federal Bureau of Fisheries to inspect the new dams and explore the possibility of building a fish hatchery to stock the lakes. Glenn C. Leach, chief of the U.S. Biological Survey's fish culture division, had pronounced the site perfect in every way, with gravity water flow, fertile fields to grow food for the fish, and an excellent clay foundation to line the ponds. The hatchery would include breeding ponds and feeding ponds to provide a large quantity of fish at a size where they could survive in the open lakes.

A big news story in the summer of 1937 was the expected reopening of the Frank C. Pavitte Lead Mine. It was near Silver Creek, a few miles farther northwest from Burnet, and although it had closed in 1930, it was set to reopen in September of 1937.

Pavitte had come from the mines of Cripple Creek, Colorado, in 1925, and (after much exploration and testing) opened his "lead mill" just before the financial panic of 1929. Prices had been rising throughout the mid-thirties, so Pavitte had been methodically reconditioning his plant and sinking a new shaft in his mine to better retrieve the lead he had discovered a few years before. Also, during the 1930s, a new section of road had been built to replace part of the original road which would be submerged by the rising waters of Lake Buchanan. Toward the end of August, he and Dave Kleen had accompanied Publisher L.C. Chamberlain and his wife (of the *Burnet Bulletin*) on a tour of the mine, which they found to be very impressive.

A meeting called by State Senator Houghton Brownlee brought representatives of Burnet, Blanco, Llano, Travis, Lampasas and Williamson Counties together in September to form the Colorado River Parks Association. The stated goal was to establish parks along the shores of the new lakes. Delegates at the meeting enjoyed a "good old-fashioned cowboy supper," consisting of "brown beans, barbecued mutton and cat fish" (with all the fixins).

The big news a couple of weeks later was a visit from new Congressman Lyndon Johnson, who (with his old boss: Congressman Richard Kleberg, of King Ranch fame) toured the two new dams and "met a number of friends at this place." The Bulletin reported that Johnson (still just 28 years old) "is rapidly developing into a useful and influential member of Congress." The article continued, "While in town, he made the *Bulletin* force a pleasant and appreciated visit." A dedication of the dams was announced for October 16, and Johnson was to emcee the event.

But some things in Burnet were more important than mere lakes and dams. Burnet had a new, lighted football field, and three games were to be played on it during the first eight days in October. The very first game played on Burnet's new field was between the high school teams of Bertram and Marble Falls. The second was between the Burnet "Town Loafers" and the Buchanan Dam "Time Killers," apparently informal adult teams from the workforces of the two communities. Tickets to the second game cost 15 and 25 cents; proceeds went to the high school team. The third game was between Burnet and Llano High Schools, and that night the new field was officially dedicated; all three games were well attended, with spectators from around the Highland Lakes area.

With football taken care of, the *Bulletin* turned its attention back to the dams on October 14 and 21. Front-page stories announced and then recapped the big event; Governor James V. Allred was not able to attend, and threatening weather limited the crowd to less than 500 people, but the dams (and the just-completed Hwy 29 bridge) were successfully dedicated. Druggist Roy Fry, of Burnet, who also served that year as chairman of the Lower Colorado River Authority, opened the ceremony by describing the role of General Adam R. Johnson in getting the dam built. "For years," said Mr. Fry, "this was known as the Johnson site." "The first sketch of the dam was drawn for him by

(County Surveyor) T.A. Chamberlain in 1895." Harold Ickes, Secretary of the Interior and Public Works Administrator under President Franklin D. Roosevelt, came from Washington, D.C., to deliver the keynote address; he was eloquently introduced by Congressman Lyndon B. Johnson.

Perhaps not surprisingly, it was Secretary Ickes who (in November) approved Congressman Johnson's appeal to extend the life of Burnet County's Civilian Conservation Corps Camp, which had successfully completed the original project at Longhorn Cavern State Park, and had been ordered disbanded. Johnson had successfully pleaded for an extension so the "CCC Boys" could build a road down the hill to a low water crossing just below Inks Dam (that project later became the lower section of Park Road 4, continuing north in Burnet County to Hwy 29).

In the meantime, an advisory board of the Texas Game, Fish and Oyster Commission consulted with about 100 representatives of neighboring counties to come up with acceptable rules for fishing in the two new lakes. Fishing would be allowed from May 15 to November 1, and strict daily limits would be imposed (6 bass, 6 catfish, 10 gaspergou, 6 crappie - or an aggregate catch of 12, excluding small sunfish, for which the limit was 20).

The *Austin American* reported in December that Congressman Johnson would be visiting counties around the Highland Lakes while he was home from Washington for Christmas. The article (reprinted in the *Burnet Bulletin*) announced that "he will visit Burnet County to assist officials in setting an extended CCC camp project into operation and the creation of a new state park linking Longhorn Cavern park with Roy Inks and Buchanan Dams."

One article in the *Bulletin*'s end-of-year review was titled, "Congressman Lyndon B. Johnson Gets the Job Done." The long article appears to be the work of L.C. Chamberlain, and not a press release generated by the congressman's office; it says at one point, "The Bulletin under its present management during a period of more than 30 years, has never been accused of publishing undeserved praise of any public officer," but continued by stating that Lyndon Johnson had completely lived up to his campaign promise to "get the job done." It listed the benefits of LBJ's success to Burnet County, focusing mostly on the recent rescue of the CCC Camp and the prospect of a scenic new loop between Burnet and the lakes.

The other article of historical interest at the end of 1937 was head-lined, "Houses are still scarce in Burnet," and seemed to be a kind of "State of the City" address by Publisher L.C. Chamberlain. The article noted that much of the construction boom was over, but empha-sized its lasting effects to the whole area. More than 300 new houses had been built in Burnet "during the past few years," and all of them were occupied. Burnet's school system had enrolled more than 700 students in the fall of 1937, an all-time record. Burnet's post office revenue was at record levels as well. The official population had been 1,055 at the time of the 1930 census; the *Bulletin* estimated a popu-lation of 1,800 in 1937. The article cautioned that business might not be as good as it had been with the hundreds of construction workers in the county, but pointed out that the newly paved highways would bring thousands of tourists to the new lakes, and predicted that Burnet would benefit more than any other town from Burnet County's new status as a tourist destination.

In addition to tourism, the *Bulletin* article opined that "with the abundance of electricity that will be generated at our very doors, small factories should, and no doubt will, be established, and our mineral properties should be developed." The article ended by saying, "Our future is before us - our destiny is in our own hands." That was 1937.

CHAPTER ELEVEN

Burnet in 1938

Adam Johnson's factory building, near the rapids which gave Marble Falls its name, was the venue for a huge party to celebrate the birthday of President Franklin D. Roosevelt in 1938. This picture was taken before 1938; the bridge visible at right was washed away in the 1935 flood.

There were few places in the entire nation where President Franklin D. Roosevelt was more popular than in Burnet County. Congressman James Buchanan and his successor, Lyndon Johnson, had both been remarkably effective in bringing New Deal money to the Highland Lakes area, and the economy here had been a rare bright spot during the national Depression. On January 22, 1938, the *Burnet Bulletin* contained a large ad announcing that a "President's Ball" would be held in Adam Johnson's old factory building in Marble Falls on FDR's birthday.

The next week's paper announced the opening of a new Adams Food Store in Burnet in the former Neuman Brothers building. Free coffee and cake would be served to all visitors that Saturday; the article described the business as "a very complete and up-to-date grocery store in every department." A small "filler" item directly below that article described modern "swing" music as sounding like "a collision between a truck full of empty milk cans and a truckload of hogs."

Publisher L.C. Chamberlain was getting a little frustrated with the reporting done by the *Austin American*. One story reported that Burnet had been cut off from Austin when the Bluffton bridge had been washed out; another said that Buchanan Dam had protected Austin from a flood on the Llano River. When a third story advised fishermen to take advantage of a longer fishing season in Llano County by staying on the Llano County side of Lake Buchanan, the *Bulletin* printed an editorial recommending that the citizens of Burnet send a map to the Austin newspaper, and pointing out that fishermen were likely to get in trouble if they heeded the American's advice, since it was actually Burnet County that had a longer fishing season.

On February 17, the *Bulletin* published an editorial to say that "Congressman Lyndon Johnson should not have opposition," explaining that he had only been in office for ten months (he won a special election in 1937 after the death of Congressman Buchanan) and that he had already proven to be more effective than most of his senior colleagues during that time.

A store called "Joseph's" (formerly Hage & Co.) announced a "re-organization sale" with some amazing deals: Ladies' shoes were just 99 cents a pair, and 21" x 40" Cannon bath towels were only a dime. Kincheloe Service Station, on Highway 66, advertised a "Life-Time Guarantee" on Firestone Tires.

J.F. Barnes and the Friedsam estate volunteered to donate land along the east side of Inks Lake if Burnet County would promise to put up fences and build a road and a park to create public access to the lake. W.E. Stevens, who owned property near the Highway 29 bridge, announced that the San Antonio Boat Club would sponsor races on Inks Lake, to be headquartered on his property.

A small March 14 news item (with major historical importance) said, "the *Bulletin* is authorized to announce Wallace Riddell as a candidate for Sheriff of Burnet County."

A March 21 article told of plans to build a "cut-off" road to connect the new Highway 29 (north of the square) with the old one, which had come into town from the southeast, and gone past the depot to the square. It would be "west of the bridge across the stream that passes through the City Park. The road will go through the city park and cut off a small corner of Mr. Shilling's property, which he has very graciously donated to the city. This road is already paved to the depot, and will be paved the remainder of the way." The project was expected to help some of the merchants who would lose business when the highway bypassed the square.

WALLACE RIDDELL

Wallace Riddell ran his first successful campaign for Burnet County Sheriff in 1938. He went on to serve longer than any other sheriff in Texas history.

That same article, titled, "Improvements Promised," listed some examples of recent progress: "several miles of paved streets, an excellent water system and a fire department of which every citizen is proud." It told of plans to build a "sewerage system," and opined that without it, Burnet "will never rank as a sure enough progressive little city."

That same March 21 issue reported that (according to Congressman Johnson) a National Youth Administration Camp in Burnet County was "practically assured," and that the NYA boys would work on projects at Buchanan and Inks Dams. A separate article mentioned a meeting on the proposed federal fish hatchery, and pointed out that the *Austin American* had wrongly reported that it would be located on Lake Buchanan. "According to information received by this office," the *Bulletin* article said, "it will be located below the Inks Dam, and will not be situated on either lake."

Some time in March, Dr. J.A. Shepperd opened a new hospital in the "Petrick Building," located just north of Burnet on Hwy 66. It was "a splendid new structure, built of granite," and was considered

This aerial photo, probably taken in 1939, shows the growing National Youth Administration (NYA) Camp and fish hatchery below Inks Dam.

to be ideally situated for "such an institution."

Buchanan and Inks Dams were finished by the spring of 1938, but Burnet's attention pivoted naturally to the new lakes that had formed behind them. The front page of the April 7 *Burnet Bulletin* featured a program for "Steve's Trophy Regatta," a day of boat races on Inks Lake on April 10, based at W.E. Stevens' property near the new bridge on the Burnet County side of the lake. There would be races for six separate categories of boat (Class "A" Service Runabout, Class "B" Hydroplane, etc.), with cash prizes for the top three finishers. There would be a "free-for-all" race with two heats, and a 12" trophy would be awarded to the winner of each heat; the overall "high point man" would get "Steve's Trophy."

That week's paper also reported that 3,000 people had attended an Open House hosted by the CCC Camp and Longhorn Cavern management to allow people to see what the CCC Boys had accomplished in the cave and above ground at the state park. The occasion was enhanced by music from the school band.

An April 21 article announced that (according to Congressman Lyndon B. Johnson) work would begin May 1 on a new fish hatchery on the Colorado River just below Inks Dam. The LCRA would act as sponsor for the project, deeding 63 acres of land to the U.S. Bureau of Fisheries, which would provide supervisors, skilled labor, trucks and material for the project. The National Youth Administration would provide the unskilled labor, creating approximately 200 jobs for eligible teenagers. Congressman Johnson explained that this project would "round out the complete CRA program," which included flood prevention, water storage, electricity generation and recreational opportunities.

An accompanying article told of a visit with A.G. Murchison, who owned the entire western side of Inks Lake and quite a bit of the Llano County side of southern Lake Buchanan. "Mr. Murchison has lived in this section for 68 years," the article reported, "growing up as it were with the country." He was "a great fisherman" who remembered when "a man could catch a whole sack of cat fish in a very short time." He didn't think that "the present day bass taste near as good as the Colorado River cat fish," and did think that "Burnet and Llano Counties should have identical fish laws."

The April 28 paper reported that J.C. Kellam, LBJ's successor as head of the Texas NYA, had announced that a Resident Training Project would begin May 2 at Buchanan Dam, the seventh such project in Texas, and would involve 150 NYA boys. That same issue also reported that the federal government had spent between 25 and 30 million dollars to "provide the finest fishing grounds in the Southwest," and would be stocking the "new Texas lakes" with 5,000,000 fish each year. The Inks Dam hatchery project would begin with 10 acres of rearing pools, which would allow newly hatched fish from the San Marcos hatchery to grow "to a size where they can safely be transferred to the river reservoirs." More pools would follow as quickly as possible, with a total cost of around $150,000 for the new hatchery.

The San Antonio Boating Association announced that the State Boat Races, an event twice the size of the recent "Steve's Trophy Regatta," would be held at Inks Lake on May 15, using facilities on both sides of the lake (Steve's Place and the Murchison Ranch) to accommodate the expected crowds. And the NYA boys began to arrive in groups at Buchanan Dam to work on three projects: the hatchery, an administration building, and a 60-acre truck garden.

Ben F. Criden was the project superintendent, and "quite a number" of the NYA boys were from Burnet County. The NYA boys organized their camp "along lines of a modern city government."

On May 12, an article headlined, "Federal Fish Hatchery Started at Inks Dam," reported that 125 NYA boys had been selected for the project, and were currently living in buildings constructed for workers during the construction of Buchanan Dam. They were beginning work on the hatchery, on new dormitories at Inks Dam, and on a new granite administration building at Buchanan Dam.

The article went on to say that the boys had been "selected chiefly from families living in small towns and rural areas. They will work about one-half their time and during the other half will be given instruction in subsistence farming and in farm shop work of such nature that they will be enabled to care properly for farm equipment and to build and repair their farm structures. A tract of arable land adjacent to the fish hatchery will be cultivated by these boys as part of their farm training, while shop training will be provided in blacksmith and woodworking." The boys would earn enough to pay for their room and board, plus about $8 per month for their own use.

Another article in that week's *Bulletin* reported that 10,000 people had attended the Inks Lake boat races in April, and that "a much larger crowd" was expected for the May 15 races. It also reported that "Buchanan Lake is getting close to the top of the dam, and makes a body of water that is worth driving many miles to see."

Commissioner R.U. Frazier completed "the cut-off road from Highway 29 through the old City Park to where it connects up with old 29 at Mannie Shilling's residence." The report added that "when Highway 29 through Burnet County is paved in July or August, this cut-off will likely also be paved."

The Rural Electrification Administration was considering a possible loan to build rural lines in Blanco, Hays, Gillespie, Llano and Burnet Counties pending sufficient co-op membership applications and easement donations. Rates were expected to be around $2.50 per month for 40 kwh, an amount which would "not only light the average size home, but it will operate several appliances such as a washing machine, iron, radio and water pump." The REA would allot money to finance the construction of lines, but not to pay for right-of-way.

On May 31, State Senator Houghton Brownlee sent a letter to the

Bulletin, expressing his delight that "in all likelihood we will receive bids during the month of June" to pave 10.404 miles of Hwy 29, from "1.5 miles west of Buchanan Dam in Llano County" to a point "2.7 miles west of Burnet." The *Bulletin* also reported that students from "Austin, Bartlett, Comfort, Cuero, Gillmer, Hockaboy, Hamilton, Leander, Temple, Willis and Maxwell" had visited Longhorn Cavern on field trips during the month of May.

Electricity was the big newsmaker (but by no means the only news) as the amazingly rapid modernization of Burnet County continued into the summer of 1938. The facts that the U.S. was still in the grips of the Great Depression and that World War II was looming large on the horizon rated only passing mention in the optimistic reporting of the *Burnet Bulletin*.

A June 2 article discussed the goals and methods of the Rural Electrification Administration, the federal entity which would finance local non-profit co-operatives made up of small rural communities and remote ranches not yet served by the private and municipal companies which provided power in most Texas cities at that time. The co-operatives would use the loans to build power lines and secure power for their member/customers, who would then repay the REA loans gradually through monthly electric bills. One co-operative would be composed of "farm people of Llano, Gillespie, Blanco and Burnet Counties." The Burnet County representatives for the board of directors were W.B. Bryson of Bertram and T.A. Warner of Lake Victor.

Texas Power & Light Co. provided electricity for the City of Burnet, but seemed very cautious about investing its resources to expand the customer base. It did agree to furnish free power for four floodlights on the Burnet square; J.B. Hyde took up a collection from the various merchants to buy "big bulbs, reflectors and wire, then donated his labor to install one floodlight on each side of the new county courthouse. This noble act accomplished two purposes: it "showed up the courthouse at night in a very effective manner," and it served as a deterrent to "pilfering from cars on the square after nightfall, which is a practice more or less indulged in by some."

Mr. and Mrs. C.D. Garrett announced the opening of their "White Bluff Cabins," perfect for those wishing to fish on Lake Buchanan. A new "Walker's Café" opened on the west side of the

Burnet square, boasting "All Modern Equipment, Tables with Linen Service for the Family, and Courteous and Efficient Service." Seidensticker's Men Store offered men's shirts for $1.49, "shirts and shorts (striped and colors)" for 35 cents (or "3 pieces for $1.00") and Wash Pants (formerly up to $3.95) for $1.49 to $2.49.

An interesting article from Seattle, Washington, told how Japanese fishing boats had invaded the codfish banks of the Bering Sea, and the captain of an American fishing boat had requested "two dozen high-powered rifles and ammunition" to fend them off. He was quoted as saying, "We have the God-given instinct to shoot straight." This is one small illustration of the tensions between the U.S. and Japan more than three years before Pearl Harbor.

The Austin Yacht Club scheduled a "Texas Racing Circuit Regatta" for July 10 at Inks Lake. There would be eight races, with cash prizes for the top four finishers in each race. The event was expected to be the largest yet at the brand-new lake.

A special issue of the *Burnet Bulletin* on June 30 advertised, "History of Burnet County -- its Resources, Minerals, Dams, Lakes, Caverns, Fishing." Much of the history was hard to read on the microfiche machine at the Herman Brown Free Library, but the headline trumpeted facts about Buchanan Dam and "Buchanan Lake." One of the articles, more legible than most, was titled, "Burnet is the Hub – Gateway to Buchanan and Inks Lakes." After highlighting the "history, scenery and healthful climate," it listed some statistics. "Burnet has a population of approximately 2,000. This shows an increase of several hundred inhabitants in the past eight years. There are 110 active business establishments within the city limits." The article continued, "Burnet has two splendid school buildings, five substantial churches, and good hotel and tourist accommodations. Its merchants are exceptionally wide-awake and compete successfully with the store-keepers of large towns."

On July 7, the headlines read, "Additional youths on Buchanan Dam project," and, "Work to start at once on fish hatchery." The stories explained that NYA youth were building a granite administration building at Buchanan Dam, and dikes for the first three fishponds at the hatchery near Inks Dam were nearly complete. The boys ("under the supervision and instruction of competent leaders") were also rearranging and renovating buildings from the abandoned construction camp to make it suitable for "permanent quarters" near the fish hatchery. The article pointed out that the boys were not only learning "simple construction," but were "also receiving some training in shop work and farm practices. A truck garden near Inks Dam is now providing a steady supply of fresh vegetables for the project dining room."

Congressman Lyndon Johnson was given credit for organizing the program, and the *Bulletin* announced that two six-room houses with natural-rock veneer would be built at a cost of $4,500 each "for the use of superintendents and permanent workers."

The Austin Yacht Club expected approximately 15,000 spectators for its big regatta on Inks Lake July 9 and 10, "when some of the nation's daredevil race boat drivers compete for trophies and cash prizes."

The Marble Falls Chamber of Commerce invited the public to a two-day "birthday party" July 12 and 13 for the "joint celebration" of the "second annual homecoming and the completion of pavement on Highway 281." There would be "Parades, Rodeo Attractions, Band Music, Ball Games, Speaking, Community Singing, Dance Each Night, Plenty of Entertainment for All, Barbecue on the Grounds, Coffee, Bread and Pickles FREE."

Wallace Riddell, who had failed to win a majority of the votes in his first election bid, placed a political ad in the Bulletin, respectfully asking for votes in the runoff election on August 27. In the ad, he said, "I am proud of the fact that I have made a clean, honest campaign," and, "If I am elected your sheriff, I hope to make you proud of my services."

On September 22, 1938, the *Bulletin* contained an editorial titled, "Looking to the Future," which started off by saying, "Within the past three or four years, Burnet has enjoyed a wonderful growth," and continued by noting that the city would vote two days later on an option to purchase the TP&L electric system and contract to buy power at affordable prices from the LCRA. The editorial urged citizens to vote in favor of the proposition, noting that a municipal power company and affordable electricity would continue Burnet's transition "from an average country village to a wide-awake progressive little city." It noted that "several miles of streets have been paved, we have secured a splendid waterworks system, money has been set aside for a sewer system," and "we have the largest school enrollment in our history." With "cheap power," the *Bulletin* opined, "Burnet should become a bright light in the firmament of the Lone Star State."

Burnet's progress continued at a brisk pace into the fall of 1938. A *Burnet Bulletin* article at the end of September reported that voters approved a proposition to establish a "municipal light plant" by a margin of 200-4. It was understood that the city would try to purchase the existing system (from Texas Power & Light); but if a sale could not be arranged, the city would build a new system of its own.

Another article told how work had begun on the long-awaited sewer system. Forty local men were employed on the project, which was expected to take six to eight months and cost between 75 and 80 thousand dollars. Much of the pipe would be buried in the middle of city streets; it had not yet been determined where the "disposal plant" would be located.

A small news item noted that Bud Cheatham, "another fine young man to enter the University of Texas," had been home from Austin the previous weekend to visit his parents, Dr. and Mrs. P.N. Cheatham.

In another triumph for new congressman Lyndon B. Johnson, the Rural Electrification Administration announced its allotment of $4 million for 28 projects in 18 states. Almost one third of that money was coming to Johnson City, where the Pedernales Electric Co-operative would use it to build about 1,718 miles of power lines to serve 3,450 customers in 15 central Texas counties, including Burnet and Llano.

Paving work began in October on another section of the new Hwy 29, meaning that the highway would soon be paved "all the way from Austin through Burnet County" and about two miles into Llano County. Paving on the "west section" was already near completion at that time. The *Bulletin* noted that "during the dry summer months, the dust on this highway has been terrible, making it very dangerous for any kind of travel," and that "the completion of the paving will be hailed with delight by numerous motorists."

In the meantime, the section of the new highway between Bertram and Burnet would be closed for construction, and traffic would once again be routed over the old Bertram Highway for "three or four months" until the work was completed.

County Agent R.J. Buchanan reported that engineers from

the Rural Electrification Administration would soon be laying out the lines "where there are two customers to the mile." More members would have to be signed up in some sections of the county before work could begin on the lines there. Ranchers who had already signed up were encouraged to try to "get his neighbor to make application." The message concluded by saying, "Anyone wishing to make application for electricity may contact Mr. E. Babe Smith of Oakalla, Mr. L.A. Warner of Lake Victor, or call the County Agent's office."

A November 1 editorial announced, "People Busy at this Place," and added that there were no vacant residences in town, and the "clamor for apartments within the past two weeks has been great."

Much of the activity in Burnet was related to construction of the new Highway 29 and the city's sewer system, which the writer cautioned would come to an end within the next few months. New tourist trade was helping the local economy, but the *Bulletin* was hoping for some "small manufacturing concerns" to come to Burnet now that the city had its "splendid water system," plus municipal electric and sewer systems.

The "Highway No. 281 Association" announced that contracts had been let for "all unpaved gaps" between Stephenville and Wichita Falls, and a contract for a new bridge over the Brazos River would be awarded within a month. Once those contracts were completed, the only unpaved sections on the entire "length of Texas" would be in Hamilton and Lampasas Counties, and those sections were "receiving every consideration" for paving in the near future.

On November 8, the *Bulletin* published a list of "Federal Expenditures in Burnet County." It totaled more than $16,000,000 since March 4, 1933. Another news item that week announced that a new automobile agency would be opening in Burnet. The Chamberlain Motor Sales Company would offer "new 1939 model Ford cars."

The "Texas Angler" magazine, published twice a month in Fort Worth, devoted ten pages to Burnet County, and featured a "beautiful aerial picture of Buchanan Dam in color" on the front cover. It called Burnet the "Gateway to Great Recreational District," and contained an ad for "Burnet, the City of the Lakes." There was also a two-page story on Longhorn Cavern (accompanied by a two-page ad).

The Pavitte Lead Mine reopened in November, and Mr. Pavitte

brought "a beautiful specimen" of lead ore to display in the window at LaForge Hardware. The *Bulletin* reported that "Mr. Pavitte has uncovered thousands of tons of lead ore, and the only thing that stands in his way for splendid success is for lead to recover its normal price."

At the end of the year, the *Burnet Bulletin* reported happily that new State Land Commissioner Bascom Giles would reappoint Burnet resident Roy Fry to the board of the Lower Colorado River Authority. Roy Fry had been the very first chairman of that board, serving as such for three years before being appointed to a four-year term on the board in 1935.

CHAPTER TWELVE

Burnet in 1939

Two notable winners in the 1938 elections were featured in the *Burnet Bulletin* after being sworn in on January 1, 1939. They were Congressman Lyndon B. Johnson, who had won a special election to replace Congressman James P. Buchanan after Buchanan's sudden death in 1937, and Sheriff Wallace Riddell, a rancher and rodeo calf-roper from Spicewood, who had spent the past decade in the trucking business around Shovel Mountain (a tiny sheep-ranching and cotton-growing community about six miles south of Marble Falls). Johnson already had his eye on the next rung of the political ladder (he was running for the U.S. Senate a year later), but Riddell remained in the sheriff's job longer than anyone else in Texas history (probably the longest in U.S. history).

In an effort to "make Texas highways safer for all motor vehicle operations and pedestrians," traffic engineer Harry B. Phillips, of the state highway department, announced in January that "all hard-surfaced roads on the state highway system have been painted with a center stripe," and an "additional line is used on curves and hills where sight distance is restricted."

Mrs. Bailey Rodgers opened a public library in her Rodgers Floral & Gift shop; the *Bulletin* hailed her "new enterprise" as something "that Burnet has been needing for a long time."

Mrs. Annie Koon was reappointed postmaster at Buchanan Dam. The *Bulletin* reported that "Mrs. Koon has been postmaster of that place since the establishment of the office several years ago, and has made an unusually efficient official."

RANKIN JOHNSON
PHILADELPHIA A's   1941

Rankin Johnson Jr. earned a tryout with the Chicago Cubs in 1939. Two years later, he was pitching for the Philadelphia Athletics.

Twenty-one-year-old Rankin Johnson Jr., formerly of Burnet (he was the grandson of Burnet County's greatest hero, General Adam Rankin Johnson; in 1938, he was a student at Texas College of Mines in El Paso) earned a tryout as a pitcher for the Chicago Cubs. His father (Rankin Johnson Sr.) was a former major leaguer who had pitched for the Red Sox, Indians and Cardinals during his career.

The Burnet Chamber of Commerce's "road committee" met that January "to determine its method" of having roads built on the east side of the lakes. Several ideas were discussed, but no decisions were made at the meeting.

Later that month, the *Bulletin* reported that the LCRA had purchased the electric systems in several counties (including Burnet) from Texas Power & Light (a deal helped along greatly by Congressman Lyndon B. Johnson), and that "Burnet will soon have a light system of its own," since each municipality would be allowed to purchase its existing system from the LCRA.

At the beginning of February, the *Bulletin* announced a "newsy new column" to be submitted each week by the National Youth Administration camp, which was rapidly taking shape near Inks Dam. The first NYA column, under the heading, "Inks Dam Overflow," reported that the Inks Dam NYA camp was the largest in the state, with about 150 boys training there. Boys were allowed to pick a trade, then spend four hours a day learning and four hours "gaining work experience." The work experience included building new dormitories for the next newcomers, building a fish hatchery, tending a camp garden and maintaining camp vehicles. There were courses in "Woodwork, Carpentry, Medical, Auto Mechanics, Cafeteria, Sheetmetal, Landscape, Machine Shop and Commercial."

The young workers had already built a new equipment storage room, lumber shed and office by mid-February. Those projects were expected to facilitate the building of new dormitories and a large recreation building as dozens of new arrivals swelled the camp's population that spring.

When work and studies were done, there were quite a few "leisure activities" available at the NYA Camp. The camp had a "recreation room," which included two ping-pong tables, numerous board games and its own library. In addition, the camp had organized softball and basketball teams, which played against teams from the surrounding towns.

Seeing some negative trends in the camp, administrators instituted a "room improvement" contest, involving inspections and grading of the rooms to be held each week. The winners would be recognized and rewarded; the losers would be saddled with KP duty. There was one room which received a perfect score in the first week's contest, but the (unspecified) reward must have been worth some effort; there was a six-way tie (all with perfect scores) for first place the following week!

The "NYA dramatic group" announced a variety show to be held February 8, which would include "songs by Grady Jones and Richard Dean," and "dramas, music and mystery produced entirely from talented artists directly connected with this project."

A front-page article on February 16 listed "Improvements on the Lakes," including "numerous houses" and other improvements on the Llano County side of the lakes. Stating that Burnet County "does not intend to be outdone," the *Bulletin* described plans for a 100-foot-wide road to connect the "new parkway road from Longhorn Cavern" with Highway 29. The article noted that the LCRA had originally planned to build a low-water crossing just below Inks Dam, but "last July's flood convinced the board that the bridge as planned could not withstand future floodwaters, and the project has been abandoned." That plan was replaced by the idea of a road "beginning at Inks Dam and going through the property of the LCRA and the Friednam estate property, connecting with Highway 29 at the bridge across Clear Creek. This road would run within a reasonable or stated distance of the lake shore with its meanders. It would have to be fenced off from the main pasture, and a fence also placed between it and the lake shore." "Such a road would make a complete loop from Burnet, via Longhorn Cavern, to Inks Dam and the lake, on to Buchanan Dam and lake and back to this place."

Another front-page story reported on a Chamber of Commerce meeting where Burnet business leaders decided to petition the LCRA for the removal of a fence around the Austin Yacht Club, which blocked access to a public park. The Chamber discussed the possibility of running a telephone line alongside the new highway to Buchanan Dam, and heard a report by the U.T. swim coach on a possible new camp on the east side of Inks Lake. The *Bulletin* called him "Tex Richards," but he was actually Tex Robertson, the founder of Camp Long-horn. In his February 1939 presentation, Tex told the Chamber board that he wanted nothing from them but their "good will," that between 150 and 200 boys would attend the camp each summer, and that (when-ever possible) all supplies would be purchased in Bur-net. The Chamber endorsed the project, and the *Bulletin* opined that "the people of this section will no doubt give every encouragement possible to Mr. Richards and his associates."

Tex and Pat Robertson founded their legendary Camp Longhorn at Inks Lake in 1939.

A very interesting article later that February told how the Texas branch of the NYA and the Texas State Employment Service had placed 930 NYA youths in private employment during the month of January. In the meantime, the NYA population at the Inks Dam camp had risen to almost 250. Several adults from Burnet were employed at the NYA camp as well. Among those were: C.E. Richardson, J.E. Robertson, R.H. Starnater, Levi K. Keel, Tony Site, Jim McFarland, and Richard Bouchard

A story from *The Llano News* became a front-page story in the *Burnet Bulletin* on February 23, 1939. It was headlined, "Landowners signing Highway 29 deeds," and it told how the Llano County commissioners court had secured most of the right-of-way for the Llano County section of the new highway, including a 155-acre tract from the Fitzsimmons Land & Cattle Company. The land had been donated with the understanding that the county would build fences on both sides of the new road.

A very interesting ad that week told of a "19-cent Sale at the White-Way Grocery" (Hwy 66 & 29). For just 19 cents, you could get your choice of: 6 bars laundry soap, 1 big Oxydol washing powders, Pure Pea Berry Coffee, 1 lb., 1 dozen Grape Fruit (large size), 1 lb. good bacon, 4 cans pork & beans (No. 2 Size), 1 Qt. Jelly (assorted flavors), 5 boxes table salt, 1 Qt. Mixed Pickles, 2 packages high-grade mincemeat, 5 packages Macaroni, or 10 lbs spuds (best grade). "1 Bottle Catsup" cost only nine cents, but "10 Lbs. Sugar" cost 49 cents. A sack of Irish seed potatoes cost $2.49.

Another article contained the transcript of a telegram from Congressman Lyndon B. Johnson, saying: "Have secured Presidential approval WPA application to construct school building, clear landscape grounds, etc. Fairland-Toby consolidated school district. Federal funds $12,084.00. Operation project will be at the discretion of State Administrator. Please advise all interested parties."

An early copy of the *Burnet Bulletin* (published on September 5, 1874) was discovered at the residence of Mrs. S.E. Vaughan in Bertram. The *Bulletin* quoted from a report in the Bertram Enterprise that said the old paper was addressed to Captain T.D. Vaughan at Cedar Mills in southeastern Burnet County. It listed advertisers from Austin and Georgetown, plus the Austin and Lampasas Stage Line and Oatman & Phillips in Llano. Burnet advertisers included J.K. Quinn, W. Smart, W.J. Moore, Jas. Rasmussen, R. Yoe, Joe Atkinson, Dr. G.J. McFarland, Whitaker & Cook (attorneys), and

and Johnson & Hammond (General Land and Collecting Agency).

A letter to the editor from someone named Charley "discussed the building of a new courthouse at Burnet, presumably the rock building torn down when the new courthouse was erected. The cost of the building was to have been $15,000. Advertising in the paper at that time was $1 per inch." The article concluded by saying, "Until the *Bulletin* office was burned, about 20 years ago, we had files that extended back to the first year of publication, 1873, but they were consumed in the flames, which loss we regretted fully as much as we did the loss of our equipment. Their destruction caused the loss of history that can never be replaced."

In a 1939 letter to the editor, W.E. Stevens announced that there would be another boat racing contest (sponsored by the Texas Boat Racing Circuit) on Inks Lake on April 30. The *Bulletin* commented that "A couple of boat races were staged on Inks Lake last spring and summer, and they drew tremendous crowds. Such is a very fascinating sport, and people come from far and near to witness the races."

Mrs. Jettie Felps wrote another 1939 letter: "There are counties and counties," she wrote, "that have public libraries, from which books can be sent out to those wanting information or desiring to have a wider reading field. Why can not Burnet County do likewise? I have several books that I would be glad to donate, and I am sure that others would also donate to such a cause. We have a fine new courthouse, and I wonder if space could not be found in it for a library."

The NYA Camp at Inks Dam was ahead of the curve on this particular issue; in the weekly "Inks Dam Overflow" column, the writer reported that "our library collection was swelled perceptibly recently with the addition of a collection of books, magazines and pamphlets covering first aid, communicable diseases and various other health problems. Also, two popular weekly magazines have been added and within a short time we expect to receive a miscellaneous collection of fiction."

Another improvement at the NYA Camp was the construction of a telephone line to Burnet. The columnist noted that "Heretofore, the only method of communications was by travel, but a direct line is now being run." The article continued: "The right-of-way has already been cleared, and the line will be strung within a short time. This telephone line will be a great aid to the camp, removing many of the difficulties of its routine operation."

The column went on to describe the "metal work" class, and added: "Our latest motion picture entertainment was a set of educational films completely covering the field of welding. The various types of this work, and the many applications of each type, were demonstrated thoroughly, showing the extensive use of welding in many of the most important trades and industries. Film entertainment for the project this week are pictures entitled 'Modern Metal Working with the Oxy-Acetylene Flame' and 'Valves: Their Manufacture and Use.'"

A good-humored "filler" item between two front-page stories said: "No telling how long Methuselah might have lived if his tonsils and appendix had been removed, and if he had used the right kind of toothpaste, gargled with listerine and smoked coughless, soothing cigarettes!"

And in a sobering "sign of the times," in March of 1939 (after Germany had taken over Austria and part of Czechoslovakia without a fight, but before the invasion of Poland) the *Bulletin* reflected on recent events in Europe. "War clouds are getting heavier every day in Europe," the writer opined, "and a general conflagration seems imminent in the near future. Just how much bluff there is in Adolph Hitler has not been ascertained, because so far he has done as he pleased in European affairs and his hand has not yet been called. As civilized nations, England and France hesitate to bring the world into war, while Hitler goes ahead and takes what he wants. That he is endangering the civilization of the entire universe is plain to every thinking person. It is impossible to deal diplomatically with Hitler."

The article continued, "A few months ago, it might have been possible to starve Hitler into submission, but his recent acquisition of new territory will make such much more difficult. It looks now like another world war will be very difficult to avoid, the contemplation of which is horrible to think about. It will be dictatorship against democracy, and should Hitler win, freedom will come to an end."

With remarkable foresight, the writer (probably publisher L.C. Chamberlain) continued. "It will be a difficult matter for this country to remain any way near neutral if Hitler appears to be getting the upper hand. The vast resources of the United States will probably win the war, should it come, whether or not we enter bodily into the conflict."

While most of Burnet County's major construction projects were completed by 1939, there were still a few loose ends to tie up, and Burnet was still growing that spring. Rural Electrification was finally nearing reality, and a Burnet Furniture Co. ad in March of 1939 was addressed "To Rural Electrification Customers." It said, "You have probably received a wiring contract" from PEC. "If there is anything that you do not understand about this contract, we are in a position to be of service to you."

A front-page article the following week quoted PEC Supervisor Lee McWilliams: "Now is the time to plan the wiring" of homes and farms. "You must have adequate wiring to get the fullest benefits from power." He added his opinion that rural customers had an advantage over city customers who had their wiring done before recent improvements in electrical service.

An article borrowed from *The Llano News* reported that Joe Fritz, from Junction, was building a "large tourist camp" on Highway 29 in Buchanan Dam. The first building would be a 40' x 80' café to be followed by ten double cabins. "All these buildings are to be of native stone, and will be modern in every respect."

An editorial commended Mr. and Mrs. Y.J. Foulds as upstanding citizens of Burnet for many years. "In horse-and-buggy days," the writer said, "Mr. Foulds was engaged in the livery stable business for a number of years." After that, "he carried an RFD mail route for about 18 years," then transported mail from the Burnet Post Office to the Railroad Depot. "Mr. Foulds has been a progressive man," the article continued, "wide awake to the interests of his town and community. He has lived a clean, good life and raised a nice family, four girls and two boys." One of his sons worked with Guthrie Drug; one of his daughters was Secretary and Treasurer for the City of Burnet.

Another personal column mourned the death of Dr. W.I. Moore, a legend in Kingsland, Fairland, Toby and Lavista (or Wolf's Crossing) and well known in Burnet and Marble Falls. The writer noted that Dr. Moore had "never had a razor on his face," but also said, "if there has ever been a man who lived the Golden rule to the letter," it was Dr. Moore. A follow-up article mentioned the loss of another old-timer, G.J. Harwell, and reminisced about meeting Dr. Moore in 1893 at

Lavista. The writer (presumably L.C. Chamberlain) noted that he had been born on the J.P. Noble ranch in Lavista, and remembered when the town had a gin, a post office and a blacksmith shop in the early 1890s. His first visit to Burnet had been in 1896, and he remarked that "there's a vast difference" from then to 1939.

An Open House Anniversary Celebration was planned by Company 854 of the Civilian Conservation Corps to be held at Longhorn Cavern State Park on April 7. In addition to tours of the camp and the cavern, there would be a softball game between the CCC team and the team from the nearby National Youth Administration camp.

An ad at the end of March announced that Granite Station Grocery was "now open for business" on Hwy 66. The store promised "first-class merchandise at reasonable prices," "cold drinks, candies, cigarettes, etc. CURB SERVICE," and added, "Bring us your chickens and eggs for better prices."

Publisher L.C. Chamberlain, of the *Burnet Bulletin*, told of a recent visit to Mormon Mill in a front-page article on April 6. He recalled a trip to the mill 52 years before, in a covered wagon with his father, his grandparents (Kincheloes) and his uncle John (the mill was where his father took wheat to have it made into flour). It was "during the week of the great sale of town lots in Marble Falls." The group swam across the pond, which seemed "much larger then than it is now." Mr. Chamberlain mentioned that it had been owned by the family of Mrs. Price Kinser for "perhaps three-quarters of a century" at the time of the article. On the recent trip, the group continued to Marble Falls, then "came back by Longhorn Cavern and made the circle into Burnet on the new Parkway Road that the CCC Boys are building from Longhorn State Park to Inks Dam. The road is not yet completed to the Hoover Valley highway, but it is easy to travel. A fine job is being made of this road, and from it may be observed some beautiful scenery."

An April article noted that "Monday morning a crew of engineers under Mr. R.S. Weber started on the preliminary line surveying in Burnet County for the rural electrification project. They have their offices in the courthouse." Eighteen four-man crews would eventually be working out of six offices in the 18-county PEC district. Staking was expected to take four months, and construction of distribution lines would begin when staking was 25% complete.

The Granite Station Grocery offered "Friday and Saturday Specials," including new potatoes for three and a half cents per pound, Delicious apples for 20 cents a dozen, a "No. 2 Can" of June Peas or Kraut, just nine cents apiece, or twenty pounds of corn meal for 40 cents.

A "bad tornado" passed through Burnet County on April 16 ("perhaps the most destructive" ever). It touched down near Kingsland, and passed through Marble Falls before heading north. It took part of the roof off General Adam Johnson's factory and destroyed the farms of Henry Hester and H.E. Hall just south of Burnet. Trees were uprooted and blown down all along the tornado's path.

A small front-page article on April 20 reported that "Topping of Hwy 29 from two miles west of Burnet to the Williamson County line was started last Saturday." The highway had been ready for paving the previous fall, but cold weather prevented workers from doing it. The article also noted that "when completed, Hwy 29 will be topped from a mile or two west of Buchanan Dam to Austin, and 66 will be topped entirely through Burnet County." It added that "Llano County is getting ready to complete Hwy 29" to Llano, but "this road will have to settle a year or two before it can be paved."

The lure of WPA money and the problem of overcrowded schools led to a momentous decision near the end of April. A $25,000 bond (which would be matched by a $35,000 WPA grant) was approved on April 25 by the voters of Burnet. The expansion plan included tearing down the 1898 limestone school, adding four new classrooms in a new wing at the 1927 brick high school, and constructing a new school building on land to be acquired by the district. According to the *Bulletin*, "many people in the district consider it folly to tear down that building, and the *Bulletin* is with that number regardless of what engineers and the State Board of Education may say or think about it. It has stood for some 40 years as a monument to education at this place, and it appears to many that it would be almost a desecration to destroy it."

The Texas Highway Department announced that it had added almost 4,000 miles of highway to its inventory during the 1930s, bringing the total to 21,870 miles. There were more than 130,000 signs on those highways, many "reflectorized" for night visibility, and more than 6,000 miles of highway now had a stripe painted in the center of the road.

EPILOGUE

Burnet has continued to grow, through good times and bad, during the eight decades since the news stories in this book were written.

Many new buildings have gone up around Burnet; new schools, churches and hospitals along with scores of new businesses and homes. In 2020 there are museums, a golf course, an airport, a football stadium, a fairbarn with a new rodeo arena – and much more. Burnet has grown into a busy modern town.

But no single decade since the 1880s has brought so many changes as those Great Depression years, and much of the town's current framework and infrastructure dates back to the tempestuous years covered in this book.

I hope you will find it an interesting read.

John Hallowell

T.O. Whitaker circulated a "subscription paper" at the end of April for the purpose of raising funds to improve the road to the lead mine in northwestern Burnet County. He argued that the new road, equipped with cattle guards instead of the tiresome gates, would improve access to the Burnet County side of Lake Buchanan. He hoped to have the work underway by the time fishing season started.

An ad for Roy Fry (Rexall) Drug Store advertised a complete stock of fishing supplies and announced the start of fishing season as May 1. Other ads announced the openings of Rainbow Coffee Shop (Morris Sample, Proprietor) and Hullum's Cash & Carry (across from Ligon Laundry on Route 66 – "Grocery Store, Filling Station and Garage."), plus the one-year anniversary of Seidensticker's Men's Store (Blue Chambray work shirts, 48 cents; tennis shoes, 69 cents).

Congressman Lyndon Johnson announced final approval of two huge projects: the construction of power lines for rural electrification (already underway) and the upgrade of the Marshall Ford Dam, which meant a huge increase in the storage capacity of Lake Travis and better flood control capability for the LCRA. The Highland Lakes area had come through the Great Depression with remarkable progress and prosperity, but World War II was about to take center stage.